# Brewing Lager

D0917507

To Anne

# Brewing Lager

**John Alexander**

Amateur Winemaker

Published by
Argus Books Ltd
1 Golden Square
London W1R 3AB
England

Phototypesetting by En to En, Tunbridge Wells
Printed and bound by A. Wheaton & Co. Ltd., Exeter

# Contents

The story of lager   1
How lager is brewed   8
Ingredients for lager   14
Malt extract   17
Adjuncts   22
Yeast   28
Hops   35
Brewing liquor (water!)   45
Let's start brewing   52
Cleaning your equipment   58
The hydrometer   62
Degrees of extract   67
Brewing with malt extract   71
Mashing with malt extract   76
Decoction mashing   83
Boiling the wort   99
Cooling the wort   107
Fermentation   112
Beer finings   119
Bottled lager   124
Draught lager   134
Serving lager   144
Glossary   155
Index   161

# Acknowledgements

Thanks to Carlsberg Tuborg United Breweries, Denmark; Dortmunder Union Brewery, West Germany; Ian Drummond, DA for the artwork; Gilbert Dallas, MBE, for his help and suggestions; Dianne Crooks for typing the manuscript; Gordon Batchelor, BSc, for the photographs.

# 1 The story of lager

Most people think of lager as a weak, pale coloured beer and unfortunately many of our 'premium' brands reinforce this view. The term 'lager' is a generic expression from the German verb meaning 'to store' and covers a whole family of beers ranging from the golden Pilsners of Bohemia to the dark aromatic types of Bavaria.

It was in Bavaria that lager originated more by accident than design, where the climatic conditions were perfect for its evolution.

For centuries, beer was brewed throughout Northern Europe and Scandinavia with a type of yeast which floated on top of the fermentation. Bavarian monks were using yeast which worked from the bottom of the vat as early as the fifteenth century. This all came about because the monks stored their brews in the cold caves and caverns in the foothills of the Bavarian Alps to prevent them from souring during the warm summer months. It was observed by the monks that such brews cleared of yeast much quicker than brews stored at ambient temperatures and the yeast remained active at cold temperatures. By continually reusing the cask dregs to innoculate future brews, the monks unwittingly cultivated a crude bottom fermenting yeast.

Before the nineteenth century, all beer was black and 'stout-like' and was often served with a considerable amount of active yeast still in suspension, which gave it a peculiar 'bite'. Bavarian beer on the other hand, was served clean of yeast because it had sedimented during the cold storage and it tasted infinitely better and so Bavaria became famous for this type of beer.

As pale beers started to come into vogue in the nineteenth century, it was noted that beer which was stored during the winter months finished up with a 'starbright' clarity and because the yeast remained active, the lager became saturated with carbon dioxide, and so tasted fresher and lasted longer. What was not understood, however, was the effects the ice-cold atmosphere had on the protein content of the beer, which precipitated out of solution more freely at near freezing temperatures. Beer which was stored in cool caves during the summer did not clear as fast and was subject to haze and so brewing was restricted to the cooler months of the year. As time went by, towns and cities expanded and so the brief brewing period was not sufficient to cope with the ever increasing thirst of the swelling population. In order to create 'winter-like' conditions all the year round, blocks of ice were cut from lakes and streams and built around the walls of the caves which meant that beer could be produced and stored all year long. As breweries expanded rapidly during the nineteenth century, the caverns were largely forsaken for specially constructed warehouses built closer to the breweries. The buildings were lined with blocks of natural ice to provide a 'deep-freeze'. Ice was also stored above the vats, supported by specially constructed strong roof trusses to provide a chilling downdraught. The 'cellars' were insulated with a thick padding of thatch-like material to minimise the escape of cold air, each exit had two doors so that at no time was the interior exposed to an in-rush of warm air. After 1873, refrigeration became the popular way to store beer although the natural ice methods continued until the 1920s. Many other countries were keen to emulate the Bavarian bottom fermentation techniques and improve the quality of their brews but they had difficulty in producing the right quality of yeast. In 1842, a Bavarian monk smuggled a sample of yeast into Pilsen in Czechoslovakia. The Czechs quickly mastered the bottom-fermenting techniques and produced a golden coloured lager with a clean and hoppy palate which became an immediate success. How little did the monk know then, that his dishonest act was to result in the birth of a beer which was to become famous throughout the world. Today 75 per cent of all beers brewed in the world belongs to the Pilsner category.

In 1801, one Christian Jacobson arrived in Copenhagen from Jutland, with a view to establishing himself as a master brewer. He took employment for a few years in a local brewery until he acquired sufficient capital to rent a brewery and set up business on his own.

His son, J. C. Jacobson, was born in 1811, the same year he started brewing. As his son grew up, he naturally played in and around the brewery, helping out now and again and no doubt getting up to mischief! He had then, the smell of malt and hops in his nose from an early age.

Christian Jacobson who started his working life as a farm lad, was determined to ensure his son had a much better start in life and so took steps to ensure he attended the newly established Technical University. He also sent him to the famous brewing town of Munich, where he was taught the finer points of cold bottom-fermenting brewing techniques by the famous Bavarian brewer, Gabriel Sedlmayr.

The more J. C. Jacobson learnt about brewing, the more he realised that Danish brewers were not very knowledgeable and so set out to improve the situation. Armed with the skills he was taught in Munich, he initially tried out a few brews in his mother's wash copper. The brews were not successful but such was the historical importance of these early experiments that the same wash copper is preserved in the Carlsberg Museum today.

The early experiments brought J. C. Jacobson to the conclusion that he did not have the right type of yeast or spacious cold cellars for successful bottom fermenting brewing.

To acquire the yeast he again travelled to Munich by stagecoach which was by no means a comfortable journey in those days. Gabriel Sedlmayr was enthusiastic about the young Danish brewer's ambitions and supplied him with copious amounts of bottom fermenting yeast. J. C. Jacobson now had the proper yeast, but he did not have the cold caverns or cellars of Munich. Copenhagen might not have had cold caverns but it did have cold vaults under the city's ramparts. He negotiated for the vaults, was granted permission to brew in them by the Royal Danish Court, and by the spring of 1846, he was producing a high quality Bavarian-style of beer. The citizens of Copenhagen were wildly enthusiastic about this new brew and everyone spoke of the 'lager from Mr. Jacobson's vaults under the ramparts'.

Demand for the new lager beer continued to grow at such a pace that he had to consider the building of a new brewery. In 1847 he bought a piece of land with the money he had inherited on the death of his mother the year before. The new brewery was built on a 'berg' or hill, and he named the brewery in honour of his son 'Carl' and on the 10th November, the same year, the first 'Carlsberg' was brewed.

Perhaps the most famous Carlsberg is 'Carlsberg Special' which could be described as a pale 'Bock' beer. It was first brewed in 1932 in honour of the visit to the Carlsberg Brewery by the Prince of Wales. Although it is in regular production, it has been brewed on 'special' occasions such as the visit to Denmark by Sir Winston Churchill in 1951 and by Queen Elizabeth in 1957.

J. C. Jacobson was a far sighted person and recognised that the new scientific discoveries taking place in Europe would have a profound influence on the brewing industries. In 1875 he set up the Carlsberg laboratory to investigate the entire brewing process. One of the most eminent scientists of the day, Emil Christian Hansen, was appointed to run the new laboratories as his expertise was well known due to his previous work with Carlsberg.

Hansen is perhaps better known for his work on yeast and the culturing of a pure bottom fermenting strain, cloned from a single ancestor. Hansen realised that many of the troubles experienced by brewers related to the instability of the crude mixed strains of bottom fermenting yeast which they used. The first task he set himself was to see if a more stable culture could be obtained from a single cell. By innoculating several samples of wort, he was able for the first time to show the various types of yeasts which affected beer in different ways. By continually diluting the various cultures in brewers wort, he was able to separate and distinguish the characteristics of each type.

In the autumn of 1882, Hansen went to Berlin to visit the famous bacteriologist Robert Koch, who taught him the use of nutrient gelatine plates for the culturing of bacteria. Hansen applied this practice to yeast and using a microscope, observed the development of a single cell into a colony of yeast. By using this method he eventually produced a pure strain of yeast. Hansen's skills were well known in Europe and he disagreed with some of Pasteur's theories on fermentation. Pasteur had argued that if wild strains of yeast could be excluded from wort, the fermentation should be perfectly healthy. Hansen disproved this by his experiments and showed that other types of brewing yeasts could also adversely affect a brew.

At the same time Hansen was experimenting at the Carlsberg laboratories, the Tuborg brewers were experiencing serious problems with their beers which remained cloudy after lagering. Tuborg had every reason to be worried as the beer which was giving them bother was Denmark's first Pilsner, brewed with local ingredients for the Danish palate by the Norwegian master brewer Hans Bekkevold. Hansen took samples of the beer to his laboratory and after analysis it showed that the Tuborg beers contained four types of yeast. One type was a healthy bottom fermenting strain, another was a type 'saccharomyces ellipsoideus' and two strains of saccharomyces pastorianus. Several samples of wort were innoculated with a single strain of each type and after fermentation and lagering, only the pure bottom fermenting strain, produced a healthy beer, the others retaining the heavy yeast haze.

The Tuborg brewery was thoroughly disinfected and they continued production of their well known Pilsner-style of beer with the new yeast culture.

Ironically, J. C. Jacobson started to experience problems with his brews acquiring a bitter taste and bad smell. Hansen was able to point out the success he had with the Tuborg brews and because of his previous knowledge of Carlsberg yeasts, suggested to J. C. Jacobson that this might also be his problem. Although J. C. Jacobson respected the important work of Hansen he put forward his own theory that it might require a different species of yeast to stabilise the beer during lagering. Hansen retaliated by separating three different strains of yeast; Carlsberg bottom yeast No. 1 produced a consistently good beer, Carlsberg No. 2 gave an equally good taste but it was not stable on storage and the other yeast was Pastorianus which in conjunction with No. 2, produced defects in the beer. Delighted with the results, J. C. Jacobson started brewing Carlsberg beer with the strain Carlsberg No. 1 on the 12th November, 1883. This strain is still used by Carlsberg breweries to this day. All this was due to the extraordinary accomplishment by Hansen of producing a pure strain of yeast only four years after he initially started to investigate the life cycle of yeast.

The propagation of yeast was a slow and tedious business and had to be carried out at least twice a month by hand so that the high quality of Carlsberg beer remained constant. To overcome this, Hansen cooperated with Søren Antonvan der Aa Kühle, technical advisor and later, managing director of Carlsberg breweries, to produce a semi-continuous yeast propagation apparatus (which is in the Carlsberg Museum). So successful were they with the design that it is still in use, although in modified form, in breweries throughout the world. In honour of the work on yeast carried out by the Carlsberg brewery, lager yeasts used throughout the world are named Saccharomyces Carlsbergensis.

The success of the Carlsberg breweries with a pure stable bottom fermenting strain and the use of refrigeration meant that lager could be brewed in any climate. As Europeans emigrated throughout the world they took with them the technology and samples of yeast so that they could enjoy the beer to which they had become accustomed. Despite the fact that every country brews lager the brew has only three main styles.

# Pilsner

The most famous of all the lager styles. It is the most imitated beer in the world, which prompted the Czhechoslovakian brewers to call theirs 'Pilsner Urquell' which means, the original! 'Pilsner', which is commonly abbreviated to Pils, is a light beer with about 4% alcohol and a pleasant hop flavour imparted by the famous Bohemian 'Saaz' hops.

It is brewed with soft water with a low salt content and is lagered between 8 to 12 weeks.

# Dortmunder

A style of lager which is not so well known outside Germany but is the principal beer type of Northern Germany.

Dortmund has long been famous as a brewing town and brewing has been practised there since medieval times. Historical documents show that King Adolf of Nassau conferred the official right to brew beer in the town of Dortmund on the 22nd August, 1293.

The introduction of ice-cold bottom fermentation in the nineteenth century produced a unique style of lager which is slightly less bitter than a Pilsner but with a fuller flavour and deeper colour. It is brewed with hard water containing sulphates, chlorides and carbonates and is lagered for 12 to 16 weeks.

# Muncheners

The beer which made Munich famous as a brewing town and includes Bock, Salvator and Wurzburger.

Muncheners are well known for their full malty palate and this is due to the fact that they are all-malt brews and have been so since the sixteenth century. The Bavarians are a conservative people and jealously guard their traditions. On the 23rd April, 1516 the Elector of Bavaria, Herzog Wilhelm IV von Bayem passed the famous 'Reinheitsgebot' (or purity law) which forbade the inclusion of cereals other than barley in brewing. This act was of course, just a ploy to protect the Bavarian barley growers and to ensure they had a ready market at the breweries. The brewers benefited too, as they were protected against foreign competition and so had a monopoly over the home market. It was only during the late nineteenth century when the rudiments of brewing were becoming understood that it was appreciated that this act of prejudice had in fact sound technical reasons for the production of full flavoured, high quality lagers.

Muncheners are full bodied, rich, dark aromatic beers, brewed with water high in carbonates but low in other salts. They are traditionally lagered for 12 to 20 weeks.

# Bock bier

Bock, which means Billygoat, is a seasonal winter brew traditionally brewed during the period of Capricorn for consumption in the spring. It originated in Einbeck, Lower Saxony, North Germany, and although it is brewed throughout Germany, it is most closely associated with Bavaria.

Bock beer is brewed from a grist of rich dextrin malts and must not by law contain less than 6% alcohol.

Dopplebock is an extra strong version which should not have less than 7% alcohol but is generally in the range 10–12%. In recent times pale bocks have come into fashion.

# 2 How lager is brewed

A variety of cereals have been used to make beer through the ages, but barley emerged as the most suitable as it is tolerant to variable climatic conditions and is an easy grain to malt. Once malted it has a luscious sweet flavour which compliments the pleasant bitterness of hops.

## Barley

Barley is a member of the Graminae family and has been one of man's staple foods for centuries. It may be Winter or Spring sown to stagger the harvest and different varieties produce crops with yields which vary from 1.25 to 3.5 tonnes per acre. European malting varieties are usually 2-rowed but 6-rowed barleys are grown world wide.

## Malting

Barley in its raw state is unsuitable for brewing as its starch and protein are insoluble and the enzyme system which will solubilise them has not yet developed.

Before barley is accepted for malting it is subjected to a variety of tests to determine such things as its moisture level, the size, shape and texture of the corns, how well it will grow, or germinate, and its starch and nitrogen content.

An important requirement of barley is that it should produce as much sugar as possible for fermentation. Just how much sugar which can be produced is generally determined as the higher the starch content the lower the nitrogen content and so a good yield of sugar. As the nitrogen content increases so the potential sugar yield decreases dramatically.

Some nitrogen is of course important in brewing as it provides yeast with nutrient and therefore helps a healthy fermentation. Too much nitrogen however, can produce colour control problems during boiling, excessive yeast growth which will produce off flavours and haze in the finished beer. It is desirable therefore that the nitrogen content is between 1.4% and 1.9%.

Once barley is accepted, it is graded into three sizes so that each batch will have even growth. The Maltster, in order to get the grains to germinate, deliberately creates 'Spring-like' conditions for the barley by steeping it in water for up to 60 hours, taking care that the correct temperature and aeration levels are maintained. As the barley steeps, it swells and softens and as the embryo starts to grow, it takes up oxygen and releases carbon dioxide.

In the traditional 'floor' maltings, the grain is drained and left in heaps (couching) and as the grain starts to sprout or chit, the temperature inside the couch will rise. If the temperature is not controlled, growth will be uneven, producing a poor quality batch of malt and the grains risk suffocation due to high level of carbon dioxide. To prevent this, the grains are spread over the floor to a depth of about 150mm and temperature and aeration are controlled by turning the grains periodically with a wooden shovel, rake and sometimes a plough.

As germination proceeds, the barley shoot (acrospire or blade of grass) feeds on the reserve store of starch and proteins in the endosperm until it is mature enough to draw nourishment from the sun and soil. In order to utilise the foodstuff in the endosperm, the shoot sends out 'gibberellins' to the 'aleurone' layer in its skin which in turn responds by producing 'gibberalic acid', a plant hormone which speeds up cultivation of the enzyme system. When the enzyme system is fully formed it continues to break down the starch and protein to feed the growing shoots.

A host of enzymes are produced which act as catalysts and 'modify' the contents of the grain so that it becomes more friable. The enzymes are grouped as 'protease' and 'diastase'. Protease breaks down the structure surrounding the starch and protein and reduces the protein to amino acids which leaves the starch accessible for the diastase to convert into sugars.

With plump 2-rowed barleys, germination is allowed to continue until the acropsire has grown just visibly under the husk, until it is about three-quarters the length of the grain and the rootlets are about one centimetre long. When this stage is reached, the malt is termed to be 'fully modified' and it is essential to halt the growth of the acrospire before it consumes too much of the starch which will eventually be extracted by the brewer. The procedure is the same for 6-rowed barleys but the growth of the acrospire is restricted so that the malt is deliberately 'under modified' but the enzyme system is fully developed with only slight digestion of the starch. To halt the growth of the growing shoots, the Maltster employs a heating process called 'kilning'.

# Kilning

During kilning, the malt is dried by passing a steady stream of hot air through the grains until its moisture content is reduced from 45% to about 3.5%. The grains can spend up to 20 hours in the kiln with temperatures starting off about 55-65C rising to 80-85 for the final curing.

The low kilning temperatures ensures the enzymes are not killed off and the grain retains a pale straw colour.

Modern malting and kilning are highly automated and the grain is kept on the move by pneumatic systems, conveyor belts, screw mechanisms or revolving drums. The moisture, warmth and aeration levels are closely monitored and each stage is controlled by the latest computer and video technology.

# Milling

Before the brewer can extract the remaining starch from the malt and convert it into fermentable sugars by mashing it in hot water, he first of all must crack it open so that the friable interior will more readily dissolve in water and allow the enzymes to diffuse throughout the mash.

The degree of milling is very important, to ensure that the maximum amount of starch is extracted without excessive crushing of the grain husk. Lager malts are milled slightly finer than ale malts. After milling, the crushed grains are referred to as 'grist' and are conveyed to a grist case, a large hopper just above the mash tun. Although unmalted cereals are forbidden in Germany, they are extensively used throughout the world to supplement the malt content. Such adjuncts are treated in a variety of ways before being added to the mash tun.

# Mashing

Mashing continues the natural process started in the maltings, but in this case the enzymes are encouraged to attach and convert the starch into sugars and the protein into soluble by-products. Because the shoots have previously been killed off, the sugars and protein residue remain in the mashing water which is eventually called 'wort', after it is separated from the mash.

There are various methods of mashing designed to extract the maximum amount of sugars from various qualities of malt.

British beer is produced by the 'infusion' method and is most suitable for fully modified malts. The mash is mixed with hot water to produce a porridge-like slurry which is allowed to stand for up to two hours at 65C (150F).

Because lager malts are under-modified, the protein content has only been slightly degraded and so it is desirable that further proteolysis takes place otherwise the finished beer might be subject to haze. Decoction mashing evolved as the most suitable method of achieving this and at the same time extracting the maximum amount of sugar.

Decoction mashing is versatile in that it is suitable for malts which have undergone various degrees of modification. Decoctions might be triple or double depending on the characteristics required by the brewer.

In the traditional triple-decoction mesh, the grist is mixed with hot water so that it settles out at about 38C (100F). After a rest of about thirty minutes, a third of the wort is drawn off and heated in a mash kettle to 65C (150F), and held there until the starch has been converted to sugar. It is then brought to boiling and returned to the mash tun thereby raising the overall temperature to about 55C (130F). After a further rest of 30 minutes, the breakdown of protein is complete and a further quantity of wort is drawn off and the process is repeated. When this is returned to the mash, it raises the temperature to about 65C and the starch is rapidly converted to sugars.

Once the conversion of sugars has been confirmed, the process is repeated to raise the temperature to 77C (170F) to halt enzyme activity. The mash is now transferred to a 'lauter' tun (Lauter in German means 'to clear') where the mash is sprayed with hot water to recover the extract.

The 'double decoction' process is an easier version and is best suited for good quality, well modified malts. It starts off about 50C (122F) and after a brief rest to restrict proteolysis, about half the wort is drawn off and brought to boiling and immediately returned to the mash. This brings the temperature up to 65C and as soon as the starch conversion has taken place, the process is repeated to raise the temperature to 77C before sparging.

Programmed infusion mashing has similar resting times but the mash temperature is raised within the mash tun by high pressure hot water heating.

# Sparging

The lauter tun is constructed in a similar fashion to a British infusion mash tun, but it is generally much shallower and sparging is assisted by propeller-shaped blades which slowly rotate and assist the run-off of worts. As the first runnings are drawn off, the grains settle on the perforated base and act as a filter. The sparge water is heated to about 80C (175F) and as it percolates through the mash, it dilutes the viscous sugars and washes them out of the grain.

# Boiling

The wort collected during sparging is run into a large boiler called a 'copper' (so called because it was traditionally made from copper) or sometimes a 'kettle'.

Boiling is conducted for up to two hours and during this time the wort is sterilised and a certain amount of protein is precipitated. Hops are added at the beginning of the boiling and their resin content is extracted to impart the familiar hoppy and thirst quenching tang.

# Cooling

After boiling, the hot wort is rapidly cooled by passing it through paraflow-refrigerators and the wort is cooled by a counter current of chilled water. As the wort is cooled, a further precipitation of protein occurs which is removed before the wort is aerated and the yeast pitched.

# Fermentation

The wort from the coolers is collected in tall cylindro-conical vessels designed to control the temperature and aeration during fermentation. The yeast utilises the wort sugars as a source of energy in order to reproduce itself and alcohol and carbon dioxide are by-products of this activity.

Lager is fermented by a strain of yeast which sediments after the

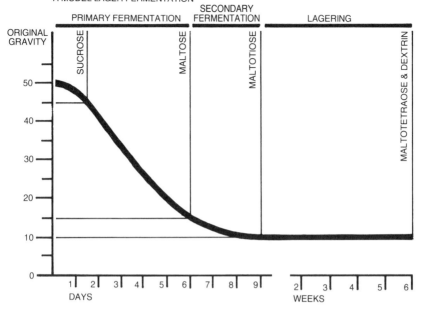

A MODEL LAGER FERMENTATION

primary fermentation. The primary fermentation might last up to two weeks and when it is almost finished, the wort is chilled to halt its activity. The lager is then transferred to large tanks, deep down in cool vaults, with about 2° of fermentable extract remaining which will sustain the long cool secondary fermentation.

# Lagering

During the secondary conditioning period, the yeast remaining in the immature beer will continue to act upon the residual sugars and subtle chemical changes take place. Finally the temperature is gradually reduced to just above freezing point and certain protein complexes precipitate out of solution so that the finished lager will be free from haze.

Further treatment by filtering and in some cases pasteurising might take place before the lager is kegged, canned or bottled.

# 3 Ingredients for lager

The traditional ingredients for lager were malt, hops, yeast and water. Although some countries still restrict lager brewing to these ingredients, many others include extracts, adjuncts and sugars.

## Lager malt

The traditional lager malt is produced from 6-rowed barley which is now mostly grown in Canada, the United States, Latin America and Australia.

It does not have as good a yield as European 2-rowed barley malts due to its long thin shape, slightly thicker husk and a higher percentage of nitrogen. Because it is an under-modified malt, it remains highly diastatic with degrees lintner up to 200, which makes it capable of utilising large amounts of mash tun adjuncts.

An important constituent of lager flavour is derived from 'dimethyl sulphide' and so the degree of kilning is controlled to encourage its presence.

## British-style lager malt

British lager malts are produced from plump good yielding 2-rowed barleys with a lower level of nitrogen in the range 1.65 to 1.75%. Kilning temperatures are on par with 6-rowed barley malts but extract recovery is slightly higher.

## Ale malt

This is produced from the same barleys used for lager malts although a lower level of nitrogen, 1.45–1.55%, is preferred. It is kilned initially between 60-90C (140-194F) and peaking just above 100C (212F) for the final curing.

During malting, the formation of dimethyl sulphide is suppressed by additions of bromates so that its flavour effects are lost in ale brewing. Although it can be used for producing lager, the true palate is restricted.

# Crystal malt

Take a grain of crystal malt and chew it and one will quickly realise why it is sometimes called caramel malt. It has a delicious caramel flavour and is produced from well modified barley which has not yet been kilned.

The moisture content of the grain is boosted to about 50% and the surface moisture is removed very quickly using indirect heat. Using direct heat, the temperature of the grains is boosted to 65-70C (150-158F) so that the diastase is activated and because ventilation of the kiln is restricted, the grains mash in their own juice. The temperature is gradually raised to 100C and during this time full conversion takes place and the grain interior becomes fluid. Finally, the direct heat is increased to between 131–138C (250-280F) and held there for up to 2 hours. During this time, the malt acquires a golden-brown colour and its interior dries to a hard toffee like mass.

# Cara-pils

This is a slightly paler, but sweeter version of crystal malt. It is made in much the same way but the final colouring and curing temperatures are much lower and the grains are roasted for a longer period.

# Roast malt

Sometimes called 'black' malt, it is made from fully modified malt which has undergone limited kilning to reduce its moisture level but has not been finally cured.

Roasting starts off about 75C (175F) and is boosted to about 150C (302F) during the first hour, then raised during the next hour to 180C (356F) and finally roasted and cured at 220-230C (428-446F).

Frequent checks are made during the last fifteen minutes or so and it is essential that the correct colour is achieved without charring the grains which can occur at 250C (480F). The malt is finally cooled by a wetting process which also allows the grains to swell up slightly.

# Chocolate malt

This is a modified roast malt kilned at slightly lower temperatures to produce a light chocolate colour. It does not have the same colouring or flavouring power of roast malt, but it does blend well with crystal malt to produce rich luscious flavours.

# Kiln-effects

As a malt is roasted, not only does its colour alter but potent flavourings and aromatic compounds are formed, its enzyme activity is halted and its acidity is increased.

Coloured malts, particularly crystal malt, contain 'reductones' which take up oxygen and therefore help to stabilise the flavour and increase the shelf-life of a beer. Coloured malts also contribute to the stability of head retention and fullness of palate.

## Buying and storing malts

Because the correct degree of crushing malt is very important to achieve the maximum extraction of sugars in the mash tun, I find it best to buy mine ready crushed. It is not possible to crush malt at home with the same success and extract recovery can be limited, plus the extraction of undesirable husk material can be leached into the wort.

The degree of crushing is not so critical for coloured malts and as only small amounts are used, adequate crushing is achieved in a food processor or blender.

A bulk buy of malt is to be preferred as a more uniform batch will give better results. A few kilograms in a paper bag will have been handled many times and if not properly stored, it will quickly go slack.

I store my malt in a large cardboard drum lined with a strong plastic bin liner. A plastic bucket with a snap-on lid would also be ideal. Small amounts of coloured malts are best stored in an air-tight container such as a plastic non-returnable confectionery jar.

Always store malts in a cool, dry, dark place.

# 4 Malt extract

Malt extract has been supplied to the brewing industry for some eighty years. Today, almost 50% of malt extract is supplied to the home brew trade, the greater amount of this going into beer kits.

## Production

Malt extract is made from high nitrogen, high lintner malts which are mashed in much the same way as in a commercial brewery. The malts are milled and then mixed with hot water to form a stiff slurry. The mash stands at 49C (120F) to allow proteolysis to take place and then the temperature is boosted to 65–68C (149–154F) to complete the conversion of starch to sugars. When mashing is complete, the wort is recovered but instead of being boiled with hops as it would be in a brewery, it is passed to a multi-stage evaporator.

The evaporators are tall cylindrical vessels designed to operate under reduced pressure. By boiling under a slight vacuum, the temperature can be kept low, so as not to destroy the enzymes or alter the character of the wort to any significant degree, but at the same time achieve rapid evaporation.

During the first stage, the boiling starts off about 30C (86F) and continues for a short period. The slightly condensed wort is transferred to the next stage where the vacuum is increased with further evaporation taking place. In the final stage, the pressure is reduced still further and the temperature is increased to not higher than 35C (95F) for diastatic extracts but might go as high as 45C (113F) for other extracts. Evaporation is continued until the wort is condensed to 80% solids.

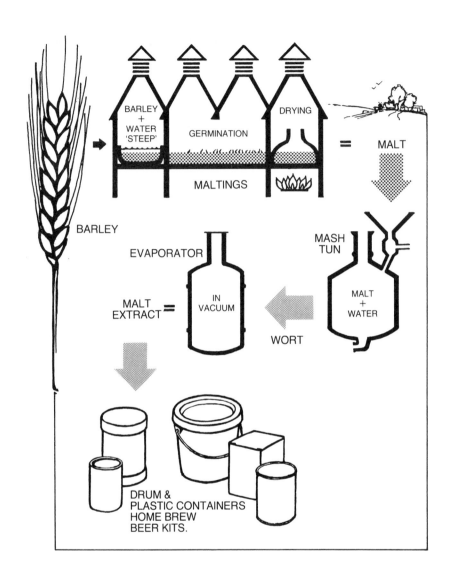

# Dried malt extract

Dried malt extracts are made by passing liquid extracts through a vacuum band drier which will reduce the moisture level to 3.5% producing a readily soluble powder.

# Liquid malt extract

| Name/type | °Lintner | Characteristics | Quantities |
|---|---|---|---|
| *Boots*<br>Plain Malt Extract | Nil | A light coloured extract with a mild malt flavour, suitable for pale lagers | 1.7 kg |
| *Munton & Fison*<br>National (Light) | Nil | A pale golden extract with a light malt flavour especially produced for Pilsners and Dortmunders | |
| Melmalt<br>(Medium) | | A medium coloured extract with a full malt flavour. Not too dark for a Dortmunder and suitable for Muncheners | 1.5 kg, 1.8 kg 15 kg and 25 kg |
| B. B. (Dark) | Nil | A very dark extract with a rich sweet caramel texture. Ideally suited for Muncheners | |
| *Century* | 100° | A highly diastatic extract with a light colour and mild malt flavour | 25 kg only |
| *Edme*<br>Superflavex | 80° | An extract with a full malt flavour due to the inclusion of crystal malt in its formulation Suitable for Dortmunders and Muncheners | .907 grams, 3 kg, 6.25 kg 12.5 kg and 25 kg |

*Paine's*

| | | | |
|---|---|---|---|
| Plain Light | Nil | A light coloured extract produced from low kilned malt. Recommended for Pilsners and Dortmunders | 1.5 kg |
| Plain Medium | Nil | An amber coloured extract with a malty texture, ideally suited for Vienna and Munich types | 1.5 kg |
| Plain Dark | Nil | A richly flavoured extract with roast malt, roasted barley and caramel in its make up. Excellent for all dark styles of lager | 1.5 kg |
| Diastat Malt Syrup (DMS) | 55° | An extract with an identical ratio of sugars as SFX, but with a light malt flavour suitable for Pilsners, and Dortmunders | |

# Dried malt extract

| Type | Characteristics |
|---|---|
| Pale | A Very light extract with light malt flavour |
| Cream | A pale coloured extract with a fuller flavour |
| Light Brown | A full flavoured extract with a delicious flavour |

| Dark Brown | A strong flavoured extract with a full malt texture |
| Hopped | Produced by Munton & Fison. A lightly hopped pale coloured extract |
| Quantities | 500 grams, 1 kg and 3 kg packs |

# Shelf life

Malt extracts do not keep in good condition indefinitely and proper storage conditions are important, particularly if large amounts are purchased.

Liquid diastatic extracts should be stored in a cool place (the warmer the temperature, the shorter the shelf life) and used within twelve weeks of purchase. Non-diastatic extracts last quite well up to twelve months if properly stored, but I would recommend that they be used within six months of purchase as we do not know how long they have been previously stored.

Dried malt extracts are highly 'hygroscopic' and will very quickly become damp and form a hard caramel mass if not stored in a cool and dry place. It is very important that dried malt extract is bought in small amounts and used up quickly before deterioration sets in.

# 5  Adjuncts

## Mash tun adjuncts

Although unmalted cereals have been used in brewing for centuries, their use has often been brought into question. It has long been argued that they were simply a means of keeping the brewer's costs down and up to a point this is true, although a lot depends on how much pre-brewing treatment they require and to what extent they are used.

Adjuncts in my view do have a role to play in brewing and as cost is not a critical factor for we home brewers, let us look at the merits of using adjuncts.

## Nitrogen control

Crude protein is a complex compound loosely expressed as 'NITROGEN'. In theory the decoction mashing process should reduce the potential problems associated with nitrogen in brewing, and in particular the haze producing protein is reduced to soluble products. The subsequent lagering period should precipitate the 'chill-haze' factions so that the lager will remain crystal clear when served.

This works well with low gravity lagers as the overall level of nitrogen is thinned out so that these problems do not occur. In strong lagers however, the nitrogen is somewhat more condensed and so it becomes a little more difficult to reduce it to less troublesome levels. A safeguard against haze therefore, is to replace a small portion of the malt with another cereal which is low in nitrogen, which will effect a dilution of the overall nitrogen content in wort.

## Head retention

Nothing pleases the eye more than a sparkling white creamy top on a lager. Well modified malt should possess all the necessary properties for a lasting head on beer but because lager malts undergo a brief period of proteolysis, some of these substances might be excessively degraded.

To overcome any deficiency in head retention, a head promoting adjunct such as wheat malt or flour should be considered.

# Running off worts

Worts might be slow to run off during sparging for a variety of reasons, such as an incorrect pH and a high B-glucan (a highly viscous substance extracted from the wall of the barley grain during malting) level in the mash. Generally however, home brewers only experience slow run offs due to the finely ground grist particles blocking the fine mesh in grain bags or the perforations in mash tun strainers.

Should this be an ongoing problem, the answer might be to employ an adjunct which will add roughage to the mash and open it out a bit, allowing for a better wash-through effect. The choice of adjunct will depend on its characteristics and the flavour it adds to beer.

# Altering character

The various textures which cereals possess offer the home brewer scope for imparting subtle nuances into a brew, although in lager brewing, these should not be too pronounced or heavy.

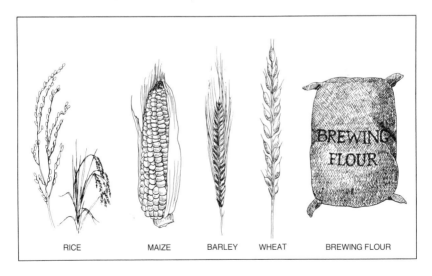

RICE          MAIZE          BARLEY     WHEAT          BREWING FLOUR

# Flaked adjuncts

Before cereals are accepted as mash tun adjuncts, they are checked for their starch and nitrogen content, how much natural oils, fats and lipids (fatty acids) they contain.

Initially, the grains are rough milled to remove the husk and further processing removes the oils, fats and lipids as they have a deleterious effect on flavour and head retention. The grains are wetted and then steam cooked to gelatinize the starch which makes it readily digested by the amylase. The grains are finally flaked through heated rollers and dried by a counter current of hot air.

# Flaked rice

An adjunct which is low in protein, colour and flavour makes it the best nitrogen dilutent and high gravity lagers can be brewed with sparkling clarity. It has fallen out of favour commercially due to its cost, but as this should not affect us at home, we should not overlook its benefits. Flaked rice will thin out malt flavour.

# Flaked maize

A good general purpose adjunct which can be used in all types of lager. It imparts a subtle corn flavour which is perhaps best suited to light Carlsberg types.

# Torrified grains

In olden times, barley was wetted and cooked in a bed of hot sand so that its starch gelatinized and swelled up to such a degree that the grain ruptured. In recent times, grains are steam cooked to achieve the same effect and successful trials have been conducted using microwaves.

# Barley

Torrified barley is readily available in home brew shops. It is a large puffed up grain which makes it ideal for opening up a mash. It has a 'nutty' sort of flavour which restricts it to dark lagers. Torrified barley assists head retention.

# Torrified wheat

An uncommon ingredient in home brew shops, torrified wheat has a bland flavour so it can be used to give porosity to a pale lager mash. It also improves body and head retention.

# Wheat malt

Wheat malt is an excellent adjunct for promoting head retention due to the amount of 'glycoproteins' (protein with attached carbohydrate) it contains. It helps produce a 'clean' grain palate in lager.

# Wheat flour

This flour is produced by processing wheat through a complex milling and sieving process. The resultant flour is readily attacked by malt enzymes but it is important to ensure that it is evenly distributed throughout the grist to ensure an even workload for the enzymes. Wheat flour is low in astringent polyphenols but high in glycoprotein which makes it ideal for a clean tasting lager with outstanding head retention.

# Grits

Grits are raw grains which undergo a cooking process in a mash kettle to gelatinize their starches before being added to the mash tun. This is not a wise procedure for home brewers as the grains might become too gummy or viscous due to extraction of B-glucan. Head retention and flavour are likely to suffer because the oils, fats and lipids have not been removed.

# Storage

Because adjuncts are only used in small amounts, bulk buying is unnecessary. Store your adjuncts in an air-tight container in a cool place.

# 'Copper' adjuncts

'Copper' adjuncts include all sugars which can be added during the boiling process.

25

# Malt extract

Malt extract provides a concentrated source of wort which makes it ideal for boilers with a limited capacity.

# Barley syrup

This is an extract made from 'unmalted' barley processed by industrial enzymes, but concentrated in the same way as malt extract. Its characteristics are similar to malt extract but without the malt flavour. It is a good wort replacement syrup for diluting the heavy maltiness of malt extracts and high gravity brews.

# Golden syrup

A concentrate made from partially refined cane sugars. It ferments well and its residual flavour creates an interesting nuance in light Carlsberg-type lagers.

# Glucose

This useful sugar is manufactured by converting maize starch by acid hydrolysis. Glucose may be bought as 'chips' or 'confectioners powder' and is only about 80–85% fermentable. Its main characteristic is to 'dry-flavour' a lager.

# Cane/beet sugars

These are the common household sugars which are made by processing raw cane, or sugar beets, to remove impurities. Further processing and refining process the familiar granules which may be bought in a variety of colours and flavours.

The characteristics of household sugars depends on the way they are treated after crystalisation has taken place. White sugar is devoid of colour or flavour which makes it suitable for nitrogen control, especially in strong beer. Coloured sugars are treated with various degrees of molasses which gives them a rich sweet texture.

Because sugar is one of the cheapest brewing ingredients, there is always a temptation, particularly by the ill-informed, to use too much of it.

This practice must be resisted! Small amounts of sugar can offer some benefits in controlling haze and reducing malt flavour, but because it is wholly fermentable, large amounts will also thin out the body of a brew, reduce head retention and influence tangy flavours in beer. About 10–15% is adequate.

## Lactose

Lactose is a sugar found in milk and is useful in brewing because it is unfermentable! It is mainly used in the production of sweet stouts but we can use small amounts of it to add some residual sweetness to Muncheners. It has about 50% of the sweetening power of cane sugar and will influence the original gravity of a beer by the same degree. Because it remains in the beer after fermentation, the final specific gravity will be higher and one must remember this when using it.

## Caramel

True brewing caramels are made by heating glucose in the presence of ammonia at 140C. It is finally concentrated to a viscous syrup, with flavours ranging from sweet to bitter. It has limited value in brewing in my view and colour adjustments are best made with crystal malt which will offer the benefits previously explained.

# 6  Yeast

Yeast is one of the lowest forms of plant life and is closely related to fungi. It has been used by man to bake and brew for thousands of years, although its precise nature and workings were not fully understood until the middle of this century. Today, yeast technology is a field in its own right and a detailed explanation of its complex structure and reproduction process is outside the scope of this book. I am not suggesting however, that had it been included, your beer would be any better as a result! Yeast is a monocellular organism, so tiny that it only measures 8 to 10 microns in diameter, or to put it another way, if a thousand cells were laid side by side, they would only measure about one centimetre. Despite being so microscopically small, yeast is a highly sophisticated form of life and its activity during fermentation is complex.

To reproduce itself, yeast works best in a fluid environment and can live with or without oxygen. A well formulated brewer's wort should contain more than sufficient nutrient to sustain a vigorous fermentation and there should be no need to add nutrient salts to aid fermentation.

As soon as yeast is added to wort, it starts to secrete a number of enzymes which will break down the oxygen and wort sugars such as sucrose, fructose, maltose and maltotriose as a source of energy and will assimilate over 40% of the nitrogenious substances in wort. The time taken from the pitching of yeast until enzyme activity is initiated is known as the 'lag' phase.

Yeasts reproduce by a phenomena called 'budding' which is an asexual form of reproduction and produces a family of the same genetic material called clones. To do this, the nucleus of the mother cell starts to divide into two and as it does so, it causes a bulge, or bud to appear in the cell wall. As the nucleus continues to divide, so the bulge will grow until the nucleus eventually splits into two and a dividing wall forms between the two new cells producing two yeasts. The two cells then separate, although further budding can take place before the daughter cell breaks away from the original mother cell. Budding takes place every eight hours or so and each cell can divide itself up to 40 times before it dies. This process continues until there are thousands and eventually millions of cells.

Reproduction is more efficient in the presence of air (aerobic fermentation) as the yeasts utilise the oxygen and sugars as a source of 'high' energy which favours rapid reproduction and the by-products are mostly carbon dioxide and water. As the oxygen in the wort is used up and replaced by carbon dioxide, the yeast switches to another 'pathway' which does not require oxygen. In the absence of air, (anaerobic fermentation) the yeast utilises the sugars which only produce 'low' energy and so reproduction is much slower, but the by-products are carbon dioxide and alcohol.

The home brewer should remember these two points as they have a significant bearing on fermentation.

# Yeast classification

Brewing yeasts can loosely be divided into 'top' and 'bottom' strains depending on their ability to float to the top, or sink to the bottom after the primary fermentation.

All brewing yeasts held by the National Collection of Yeast Cultures have their characteristics tested and rated as follows:

(a)     The amount of yeast at the surface during fermentation.
(b)     The amount of sedimented yeast after the primary fermentation.
(c)     The degree of attenuation.
(d)     The rate of attenuation.
(e)     How quickly the beer clears after fermentation.

Each activity is rated on a scale ranging from 1, which gives the poorest results, to 5, which produces the best results. The majority of home brewing lager yeasts have the following characteristics:

(a)     1, showing limited surface activity.
(b)     5, a good deposit of sedimented yeast.
(c)     5, utilises the maximum amount of wort sugars.
(d)     4/5, a good steady rate of fermentation.
(e)     5, excellent clarity in the finished beer.

# Dried yeast

Dried yeast is produced by propogating a single cell with the desired characteristics in a nutritious wort-like solution. The culture is allowed to grow until there is about 500 grams of it, when it is checked to ensure the cells have not become contaminated with wild yeasts or bacteria. If all is found to be well, the sample is transferred into the smallest of three propogating vessels under strict sterile conditions. In this vessel, the rate of feeding is increased and nutrients and air are injected at an increasing rate to match the growth of the yeast. The air is made sterile by passing it through a series of filters of ever decreasing size, so small that even the smallest of micro-organisms are prevented from passing. The air is compressed and chilled and passed through the medium in very small bubbles to encourage absorbtion.

After the yeasts have outgrown the first vessel, they are transferred to the next biggest where the process is continued. Eventually, the yeasts are passed to the biggest and final vessel where the rate of feeding is speeded up and the final rate of aeration is increased to several thousand cubic feet per minute!

After a period, several tonnes of yeast is produced and harvested by passing the yeasty fluid through centrifugal separators which remove most of the water to leave a thick paste of about 15% solids. The paste is further treated by washing it with pure water to remove all residual sugars and nutrient. It is then passed through rotary vacuum filters which further reduces the water content to leave the yeast in a semi-solid putty-like state. Finally the yeast is dried under controlled conditions on a fluid bed system so that the resultant dried granules remain in active form.

# Lager yeast

Lager yeast, Saccharomyces Uvarum (formally S. Carlsbergensis) is a pure strain cloned from a single ancestor and is classified as a bottom fermenter as it sediments after the primary fermentation.

Depending on its characteristics, it might be strongly sedimentary, in which case rousing might be necessary to keep the yeast in suspension to ensure a satisfactory degree of attenuation. Some strains may be a little more powdery, remaining in suspension longer and so produce a steady rate of attenuation with resort to rousing.

True lager yeasts have the ability to completely utilise the trisaccharides 'melibiose' and 'raffinose' whilst 'ale' yeasts do not. They are also capable of fermenting at much lower temperatures than ale yeasts and it is this characteristic which makes them most suitable for lager.

# Home-brew lager yeasts

The following yeasts are readily available in home-brew shops.

# Vibrka lager-bier yeast

One of the best lager yeasts available, it is produced by Friedrich Sauer in cooperation with world-famous German Breweries. It is available in dried or liquid form and imparts a true lager character. It is an excellent yeast for the true lagering process.

# Vibrka Munich-bier yeast

A culture ideally suited for aromatic Muncheners and Bock-style beers. It also proved interesting in Irish stout!

# Glenbrau quick-acting Danish yeast

A strain which certainly lives up to its 'fast' fermenting claim. It is quick to activate from the dried state and ferments well with a fast, but steady rate of attenuation. It is a clean tasting yeast which does not influence beer flavour to any significant degree.

# Home gourmet

A liquid culture cloned from a true lager strain which should give consistently good results.

# Yeast starters

A yeast 'starter' should always be considered for the following reasons:
To pitch vigorously working yeast to wort, to encourage a quick fermentation and reduce the chances of bacteria infecting the brew.

To activate the small amount of yeast in liquid cultures and to propogate them to provide an adequate amount of cells to ensure a healthy fermentation.

# Dried yeasts

Dried yeasts can usually be activated and pitched into wort in a few hours. Do not be too hasty however, as good results will be achieved by leaving the starter to grow overnight.

To make up the starter, boil 285 ml (10 fluid ounces) to sterilise it and dissolve in it one tablespoon of malt extract. Allow to cool to 20C (68F), pour it into a suitable container and shake it vigorously to aerate the solution. Add the yeast and again shake and agitate the container to help dissolve the granules and leave in a warm place until the starter is positively active.

# Liquid cultures

Increase the water to 500 ml ($^3/_4$ pint) and boil as before, dissolve three tablespoons of malt extract in it and cool to 20C. Shake the phial or sachet containing the liquid yeast to dislodge it and add to the solution. Give the starter bottle a good shake to mix in the yeast and aerate the medium, fit an air-lock and leave in a warm place for at least 72 hours.

The fitting of an air-lock will deny the yeast access to air which is, as I have previously explained, necessary for rapid yeast growth.

However, because the starter is to be left for three days before it is used, it must be protected from infection. Aeration therefore, is supplied by giving the container a vigorous shaking at least twice a day to drive off the dissolved carbon dioxide and replace it with some oxygen.

# Reusing yeast

In commercial lager brewing, the yeast for re-pitching is taken from the centre layer of deposited yeast sludge. It is cleansed in pure water to remove dead yeasts and bacteria and repropogated in a wort solution before re-pitching.

It is not advisable for home brewers to attempt this practice as we cannot be certain about the health of the yeast. All is not lost however and the following procedure can give good results.

*Active yeast starters ready for pitching.*

When the wort has attenuated to 1010, draw off a 250ml sample into a sterilised container. Give the wort a good shake to drive out the carbon dioxide, seal the container and place it in your refrigerator. The sudden chilling of the wort sample will halt the yeasts activity and cause it to sediment, although some cells might flocculate to the surface and they should be removed. A teaspoon of the sedimented yeast can now be re-propogated.into a viable culture.

Should you ever be in any doubt about the quality of the yeast, it is wise to discard it and propogate a new culture.

# 7   Hops

Hops were introduced into Britain on a commercial scale by Dutch traders during the reign of Henry VIII.

Historically, English 'ale' brewers did not brew with hops but used a variety of herbs, including nettles and bogmyrtle. When the hop was first introduced, it was initially treated with indifference, but as soon as its use in brewing started to gain popularity, the whole issue blew up into a bitter controversy which started the first Campaign for Real Ale! The hop however, with its superior flavour and preservative properties eventually won, although it was not fully accepted until the Industrial Revolution.

The first hop gardens were planted near Ashford and Canterbury in Kent in 1520. A flourishing hop industry was soon established in Kent, which is still the best known hop growing county today. Hop growing quickly spread to the neighbouring counties of Sussex, Surrey, and Hampshire, eventually spreading to the West Midlands in Herefordshire and Worcestershire. Hop growing eventually spread to Wales and as far North as Aberdeen in Scotland and although hops are no longer grown in these countries, remnants of this popular industry can still be found growing wild in hedgerows and quiet byways.

## Cultivation

The hop plant, Humulus Lupulus, is an attractive and fragrant herb which belongs to the Cannabinaceae family and is related to the nettle.

It is a climbing perennial which produces a fresh bine each year. New plants are cultivated under artificial conditions and are planted in late June so that they can establish themselves for the next season's harvest.

Hop gardens are laid out in orderly regimented rows about 2 metres wide and the plants, called 'hills', are spaced between 1 and 2 metres apart. The growth of the hop is supported by an elaborate pole and wirework system which supports a coir stringing arrangement. The stringing method varies from area to area and might be the 'umbrella' system which uses four strings for the young shoots to grow up; or the 'Butcher' method which uses three strings or the 'Worcester' arrangement which only uses two strings.

Hops can grow to a height of 5 metres or more and so the wirework system must be strong enough to support the full weight of the fully grown hops and withstand the buffering effects of wind and rain.

The pole and stringing arrangement is very expensive to instal and maintain, which has lead to research into 'dwarf' varieties that will only grow to a height of 2 metres. This should make maintenance and harvesting cheaper and easier and perhaps in the not too distant future, all hops will be dwarf varieties.

Hops grow best in a well drained nutritious soil which will provide nourishment for the rapidly growing shoots as they spiral clockwise up the coir string. Fertilisers are added in careful amounts throughout the growing period to ensure a healthy crop. In the Spring, the young hops are trained and dressed, the most healthy bines are selected and the remainder are pulled out. Depending on the variety, there might be one, two or three bines per string. Spraying against disease is regularly carried out and the excess growth from the base of the bine is removed by chemicals to reduce the chance of attack by soil-borne bacteria.

The hop is dioecious, but it is the female which provides the fruits with brewing value. The hops are in bloom for about three weeks and are fertilised by a few male plants scattered throughout the garden. By September the hop is fully mature with a heavy crop of seeded hop cones.

English hops have traditionally been fertilised and seeds can contribute up to 25% of the weight of the hop cone. Continental hops on the other hand are grown seedless and as seeds have no brewing value, British growers are obliged to follow suit if they want to become successful exporters. Many British brewers however, prefer seeded hops and in any case some varieties such as the Golding and Fuggle do not produce good crops when grown seedless. For the English hop growers to remain successful, it is essential to satisfy the home trade and compete in world markets and so new varieties are grown with and without seeds.

# Picking

Traditionally, all hops were hand picked by local people and hundreds of 'East Enders', whose annual migration to the hop growing counties was regarded as a holiday. The pickers worked in small groups, usually being members of the same family and it was not uncommon to come across three generations in the same team.

In manual picking, the string supporting the bine is cut and the bine laid out so that the pickers could pluck the cones clean from the bine without damaging it. The cones were collected in wicker or canvas baskets and then measured into ten-bushel sacks, called pokes, then taken to the oast house for drying. The bine was left to wither and supplied the rootstock with some nourishment before being removed.

Hop picking machines were first tried out in the 1930's, but hand picking continued until the early 1960's and today all hops are machine picked. In mechanised picking, the whole bine is cut down and fed into a machine which can strip several thousand bines per hour.

# Drying hops

As soon as the hops are harvested, it is essential they are dried as soon as possible to enhance their keeping qualities.

Traditionally, hops were dried in an 'oast' which was usually a circular building with a conical roof and a wind cowl. They are a familiar sight in hop growing counties and were introduced from Flanders over 400 years ago. Today, hop drying takes place in modern factory-type buildings and although the design of the oast has changed, the skill of the hop drier has not.

Hop drying is a skilled craft and demands constant attention. Hops contain about 80% moisture and the aim of drying is to reduce this to about 8% or so by blowing hot air from an oil burner gently through the hops with electric fans. It was usual to burn sulphur in the oast to help preserve the hops and stabilise their colour but as this did not meet the approval of all the brewers, its practice ceased in 1980. Brewers who prefer sulphured hops, however, are free to carry out the practice.

When the hop drier is satisfied that drying is complete, the hops are scooped into cooling chambers with special shovels called 'scuppets' which are made with a wooden frame and covered with canvas to prevent damaging the fragile hops. The hops are initially left in heaps until the moisture level has stabilised and then shovelled through a hole in the floor into large hessian sacks called 'pockets'. The pocket is slung beneath the opening by two canvas straps and when it is full of hops, they are mechanically pressed tight. The procedure is repeated until the pocket is tightly packed with hops and it is finally sewn up. Traditionally, English hops were weighed in 'centals (100lbs) or 'hundredweights (112lbs) but today we use the European measurement of 'zentners' which equals 110lb.

# Diseases of hops

The hop industry has perhaps suffered more from disease than other farming industries. Growing hops are susceptable to a variety of pests, fungi and viruses which can very quickly cause havoc with the harvest. Disease can only be kept under control by spraying the crop with chemicals and being vigilant to spot an attack at an early stage.

Verticillium Wilt is a fungal disease which is dreaded by growers as a bad attack can wipe out years of investment. There is no known cure for wilt and should a garden become infected, the bine must be cut down and burned. In severe cases, the rootstock is grubbed up and the soil sprayed with chemicals and left fallow for years.

Over the past twenty years or so, 'new' varieties have been cultivated which can tolerate wilt and so its worst effects are manageable. Just recently, however, it has been reported that a 'super-virulent' strain has emerged which is causing concern and so urgent research is taking place on how best to counteract its devastating effects.

Mildew is another serious disease of which there are two types, 'powdery' and 'downy'. Both can wreak havoc in a hop garden and at best they can only be kept at bay by spraying with chemicals throughout the growing season. Some new varieties can resist mildew but unfortunately some types of hops can be infected without showing any symptoms.

If the foregoing diseases were not enough for the poor hop to contend with, it is also attacked by 'aphids'. The aphid, or hop-fly, survive on hops by drawing nourishment from the sap of the bine and by doing so become infected with the 'nettlehead' and 'split-leaf blotch' viruses which they unwittingly transfer to other hops.

A variety of pest can also be troublesome for hop growers. The hop flea beetle and red spider are controllable with insecticides but new super strains appear from time to time which means constant research into finding better types of chemicals to combat them.

# Parts of the hop

The hop flower forms a conical inflorescence called a 'strobil', the stem of the strobil is the 'strig' to which the petals or bracts and bracteoles are attached. The seeds and 'lupulin' gland are formed at the base of the bracteoles where it joins the strig and they are easily seen by gently prising open the petals. The seeds have no brewing value but the lupulin gland contains the important brewing resins which gives beer its pleasant bitterness, antiseptic properties and enticing aroma.

The resins are divided into two, hard and soft. It is the soft resins which are important in brewing and consist of alpha acid (Humulon) and beta acid (Lupulon). The alpha acids are the principal bittering material and hops are analysed and sold according to its level. Hops which are high in alpha acid are known in the trade as 'alphas' to distinguish them from low acid but aromatic varieties.

The 'essential' oils of hops give beer its pleasing aroma and although much research has gone into producing hops high in alpha acid (super-alphas), aroma hops such as Hallertuar and Golding are included in the breeding trial to maintain this very important bouquet.

# Hop products

Traditionally, the dried hop cones were added to the copper to extract their bitterness but today only about 40% of the crop is used in this way, the remainder is processed into pellets, powders and extracts.

# Dried hop cones

Home brewers usually refer to these as 'whole' hops. The quality of cone hops available to the home brewer does tend to vary somewhat and we should seek out the freshest batch possible. Grade 1 hops should look bright and fresh and possess a pleasant, healthy hop aroma.

Old hops look 'old', dull and lifeless. They crumble easily when handled and might have a 'cheesy' aroma. If there is any doubt about the quality of cone hop, then I suggest you buy pellets instead.

# Pelleted hops

Pellets are produced by passing cone hops through a hammer milling process and finally sieving the fragments to remove the bulk of the strig and petals, to leave a concentrated form of whole hops. The collected fragments are then mechanically pressed into pellets and sealed in small

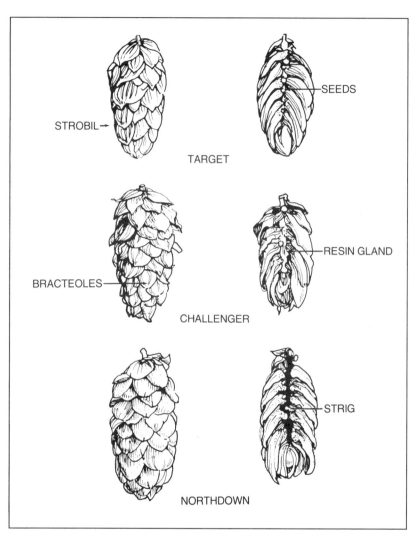

STROBIL→

SEEDS

TARGET

BRACTEOLES

RESIN GLAND

CHALLENGER

STRIG

NORTHDOWN

sachets under an inert gas to preserve them. The hopping rate of pellets is about 50% of cone hops.

## Powdered hops

These are produced in a similar fashion to pelleted hops but with a greater degree of crushing and sieving. The resultant powder contains the important brewing resins.

# Extracts

Extracts are made by treating hop cones with liquid carbon dioxide under pressure at just above freezing point. This method of extraction is extremely efficient and the extracts produced are fully utilised during boiling.

There are two types of extracts, 'standard' and 'isomerised'. The standard extract requires to be boiled as for cone hops and can be used as a partial or complete replacement for whole hops. The recommended dose is 15 ml per 5 litres ($\frac{1}{2}$ fluid oz/gallon).

Isomerised hop extract has been treated in such a way so that the alpha acids are converted, or isomerised, into 'iso-alpha' acids which are more soluble and bitter. Isomerised hop extract should not be added to the copper but can be added before or after fermentation. The dosage is about 8 to 10 drops per 5 litres and is more fully utilised if it is added 'after' fermentation.

# Hop oil

This is the essential oils of hops which impart a fine hoppy aroma in beer. It is separated from the resins by liquid carbon dioxide or steam distillation. It is an excellent product which can be added to beer in various amounts to influence the aroma and character.

As far as I know, hop oil is not sold with any instructions on how much of it should be added to home brewed beer. To work out some sort of scale for its use, I took the bold step of adding $\frac{1}{4}$ teaspoon to 23 litres. The resultant brew was drinkable, but had a strong hoppy and somewhat flowery taste. The next step was to find out the number of drops it took to fill a $\frac{1}{4}$ teaspoon and in my next brew I added 50% of that number which was satisfactory.

The type or size of the dropper used to measure the oil is not important, although a small dropper will give a greater number of drops and so finer control is achieved during experiments. The dropper which I use came from a Clinitest sugar measuring kit which diabetics use and which I have previously used in the production of sparkling wines.

# Hops for lager

Home brewers have always assumed that to brew lager, it was necessary to use continental hops. Nothing could be further from the truth! Denmark for example does not grow hops, but imports them from many countries including England. Should German growers have a poor year, they import English 'alphas' to maintain the high quality of their brews and one continental lager brewed in Britain under licence uses English hops to the complete satisfaction of the parent brewery. In any case, almost a third of all the hops grown throughout the world have their 'roots' at the Hop Research Centre at Wye College, Kent. All we home brewers have to do is come to terms with these facts and think 'English' hops! Of course, I am not suggesting that we should not use continental hops, as home brewing is for fun and by blending home grown and foreign hops, superb flavour combinations can be produced.

# English hops
## Goldings

The Monarch of the brewing industry, Goldings, have a long and proven record as a fine flavoured hop with a pleasant aroma. Their excellent characteristics are suitable for all types of lager.

## Northdown

A relative of Northern Brewer, Northdown is an excellent dual-purpose hop suitable for pale and dark lagers.

## Challenger

An excellent all-purpose hop with a clean fresh enticing aroma. It has a consistent alpha acid content and has proved its worth in pale lager.

## Zenith

Related to 'Yeoman', Zenith hops possess a high alpha acid content with good flavour and aroma, which makes it suitable for all styles of lager.

## Yeoman

A variety rich in alpha acid which is recognised as an excellent all-round lager hop, with a good aroma suitable for late hopping.

## Target

One of the most successful of the new varieties. Target is very popular at home and abroad because it is substantially rich in alpha acid but with a pleasing aroma which makes it a good all-round hop.

# Czechoslovakia

## Saaz

The famous hop of Bohemia which is considered to be the best choice for true Pilsners. It has a most desirable aroma which is much sought after and as much as 80% of the Czech harvest is demanded by the rest of the world.

# Germany

## Hallertaur

Grown around the town of Au in the Hallertau district of Bavaria, Hallertaur hops are famed for their pleasing flavour and enticing aroma. Hallertau Northern Brewer is closely related to our own Northern Brewer.

# Yugoslavia

## Styrion goldings

A relative of the English 'Fuggle', this pleasantly flavoured hop possesses a desirable aroma which is suitable for pale and dark lagers.

## Storing hops

The quality of hops does not remain stable during storage. The effectiveness of the resins, in particular the alpha acids, can deteriorate by so much as 50 per cent. This loss can be minimised by storing hops in the freezer.

Pelleted hops are protected by an inert gas and so do not deteriorate as fast as cone hops, but none the less, cold storage is desirable. Hop extract is a more stable product and offers a consistent degree of hop bitterness. It too should be kept in the refrigerator to minimise the effects of daylight.

| Variety | Average alpha acid |
|---|---|
| Goldings | 5.3 |
| Northdown, seeded | 8.0 |
| Northdown, seedless | 10.4 |
| Challenger, seeded | 7.7 |
| Challenger, seedless | 9.2 |
| Zenith, seeded | 9.3 |
| Zenith, seedless | 9.9 |
| Yeoman | 10.9 |
| Target | 11.2 |
| Saaz | 5.5 |
| Hallertaur | 7.5 |
| Styrion Goldings | 7.9 |

# 8 Brewing liquor (water!)

The manner in which certain types of water influenced a particular style of lager was recognised but not fully understood for centuries. This led to areas becoming noted for a certain type of beer and so Munich became renowned for its dark aromatic lagers and Pilsen achieved world acclaim for pale lagers.

## Types of water

An important requirement of brewing water is that it should be as wholesome as drinking water and as we home brewers use our domestic supply, this is guaranteed.

## Soft water

Soft water is the best all-round brewing water as it makes a good base to which other salts can be added. In its natural state, it is ideal for brewing Pilsners.

## Hard water

Hard waters contain all manner of salts which can impart all manner of characteristics, ranging from fullness to harshness. Untreated hard waters will not produce a fresh clean tasting Pilsner, but in dark Munich types, its flavours are at worst disguised, at best, complimented.

## Temporary hard waters

Temporary hard waters support a fair amount of calcium carbonate and bi-carbonate, which laymen describe as chalk. It is not a stable chemical

45

during boiling and it readily precipitates out of solution, hence the expression 'temporary' hard. In its natural state it is excellent for Muncheners and Bock styles of beer as the alkalinity of the chalk 'tempers' the acidity of the roast malts and the overall quality of palate is fullsome and most agreeable.

Should a Pilsner be brewed with this type of water, it will lose its freshness and clean flavour, and so the carbonate should be removed.

A Dortmunder on the other hand can tolerate temporary hard water as long as the carbonate content is not too high. Generally, however, it is wise to remove the carbonate.

# Permanently hard water

These waters support large amounts of sulphates which is mostly calcium with lesser amounts of magnesium. Carbonates are also present in considerable amounts. Calcium and magnesium sulphates are highly soluble and are largely unaffected by boiling, remaining in the water keeping it 'permanently' hard.

This type of water is unsuitable for Pilsners and Dortmunders unless the level of hardness can be reduced substantially. Muncheners too will benefit if the hardness is reduced a little but this will largely depend on your own preference.

# Types of salts

All salts in water react in various ways during the brewing process, offering benefits and disadvantages. Calcium sulphate and calcium carbonate are the most important because they have the opposite effect on the brewing reactions and so it is a good idea to look at them in some detail.

# Mashing

Calcium sulphate reacts with malt phosphate and precipitates calcium phosphate to leave acid phosphate in solution. The acid phosphate increases the mash acidity (lowers the pH) to a value which will benefit the diastase and consequently a good extraction of sugars. The pH is closer to the value required by the proteolytic enzymes and so a good separation of wort protein is achieved with excellent clarity in the finished beer.

Calcium carbonate on the other hand, decreases the mash acidity (raises the pH) away from the value required for successful mashing. This results in a poor extraction of sugars, less separation of protein and so the clarity might suffer.

# Sparging

Calcium sulphate reduces the extraction of polyphenols and so the flavour and colour of the beer remains stable. It restricts the leaching out effect of harshly flavoured materials from the malt husk and helps the wort to run free as sparging proceeds.

Calcium carbonate produces darker shades in beer, extracts more bitter substances and might restrict the flow of wort.

# Boiling

Calcium sulphate causes a further precipitation of phosphate and consequently a reduction in the pH which encourages the coagulation and eventual precipitation of protein (the hot break). The colour of the beer remains stable. It also slows down the conversion of alpha acids to bitter iso-alpha-acids and so more hops are required to bitter the beer.

Calcium carbonate will influence a rise in the pH and so restrict the hot break. A better extraction of hop bitterness is achieved but with a disagreeable harshness. The colour of the beer might increase due to reactions with polyphenol.

# Fermentation

Calcium sulphate encourages yeast to flocculate, although, to what degree might depend on the characteristics of the yeast. Because the reactions calcium sulphate has set up during the foregoing processes, the acidity of the brew continually increased which helps the beer to resist bacterial attack. Calcium sulphate influences good head retention.

As calcium carbonate counteracts acidity, the brew is susceptible to infections, particularly the lactic acid bacteria.

# Other salts

Magnesium sulphate (Epsom salts) has less influence in lowering the pH in the mash tun and indeed if present in high concentrations, will restrict the precipitation of calcium phosphate, delaying the breakdown of protein. It makes amends however during boiling, where it encourages a further precipitation of hot break. It is a valuable source of yeast nutrient but can impart a bitter astringent taste in beer if present in large amounts.

Sodium chloride (common salt) is a readily available source of chloride to help produce palate fullness in Munich-type brews. It should only be used in small amounts in lager brewing and as most water supplies usually have sufficient amounts naturally dissolved in them, it should not be necessary to add any more. Too much sodium chloride in the brewing water will produce a harsh hop flavour and a sour and salty palate.

Potassium chloride is an excellent alternative to sodium as it does not produce the flavour defects described above and because it is a health promoting salt, it should be preferred.

Calcium chloride will influence mash acidity and so counteract the adverse effects of carbonate. It is therefore a good substitute for sodium to bring out the palate fullness in dark lagers.

# Dealing with hardness

Generally, the overall need in brewing water, will be to reduce its hardness and in particular, the removal of carbonate.

# Boiling

The easiest and safest methods of removing carbonate is by the time honoured method of boiling.

Boiling moderately chalky water vigorously for 30–40 minutes will reduce the carbonate level to about 5 grains per gallon (71 mg/lt) which is insignificant. Should the water be required for Pilsners the addition of 50 mg/lt of calcium sulphate should bring the pH value within the range for successful mashing. This should be added before boiling commences to encourage a better precipitation of chalk.

Should the water be very hard and you decide to brew a Munchener the addition of calcium chloride will assist the drop out of chalk but at the same time, leave some chloride in the water which will bring out the palate fullness.

# Lactic acid treatment

Lactic acid can be used to neutralise carbonate and it will produce a 'soft' palate in lager. For accurate control, it is necessary to titrate an exact amount of carbonate with the acid so that an exact dose can be worked out. This is beyond the scope of most home brewers, but because lactic acid is safe acid, some crude experimentation should bring good results. It is available in liquid form from home brew shops but it is very hygroscopic and will rapidly take up atmospheric moisture and so the container should not be left open for any length of time.

# Diluting

The above procedures should adequately take care of the troublesome carbonate but it will not reduce the level of permanent hardness. Provided the level of permanent hardness is not too high, a satisfactory lager can be brewed but generally, best results will be achieved when it is reduced a little.

The only practical way to reduce the level of permanent hardness is to dilute your domestic supply with rainwater. This is not too daunting a task as first might appear, particularly with the British climate!

To collect rainwater, sling up a sheet of polythene to form a chute-effect to run the rainwater into a wide open topped container such as a fermentation vessel.

Never store rainwater for more than a day or so, and always boil it before use.

# Degrees of hardness

Most brewers recognise the hardness of their water supply by observing the 'fur' which collects around the heating element of their Bruheat. This is mostly carbonate deposits which have built up over a period of time.

For a more accurate assessment, a water analysis table should be acquired from your local Water Authority. It is a complex document but the part which is of interest to us is the 'Total Hardness'. This should be expressed in milligrams per litre. The following chart shows the degrees of hardness in various waters and the brews they are best suited for.

| Mg/Lt (P.PM.) | Water | Generally suited for |
|---|---|---|
| 0 – 100 | Soft | Pilsners |
| 100 – 200 | Med Soft | Dortmunders |
| 200 – 400 | Med Hard | and Muncheners |
| 400 – 600 | Hard | Dilute for all |
| Over 600 | Very hard | lagers |

# Water treatment

There cannot be a precise laboratory-like chart for the treatment of brewing water due to the varied geological make up of the country. Water authorities often switch reservoirs to balance supplies and so the salt content will vary. The home brewer therefore, should experiment so a compromise is made between achieving a satisfactory mash tun acidity of about pH 5 to 5.5 without incurring any harshness in the flavour of the brew.

The following chart should produce satisfactory results.

## A guide to water treatment for 23 litres (5 gallons)

| Water | Pilsner |
|---|---|
| Soft | Add 1 tsp calcium sulphate |
| Medium soft | No treatment |
| Moderately hard | Boil to remove chalk |
| Hard | Dilute 25% with rainwater |
| Very hard | Dilute 50% with rainwater |

| Water | Dortmunder |
|---|---|
| Soft | Add $1\frac{1}{2}$ tsp calcium sulphate |
| Medium soft | Add 1 tsp calcium sulphate |
| Moderately Hard | Add 1 tsp lactic acid |
| Hard | Boil to remove chalk |
| Very hard | Dilute 25% with rainwater |

| Water | Muncheners |
|---|---|
| Soft | Add $\frac{3}{4}$ tsp chalk $+$ $\frac{1}{2}$ tsp Potassium Chloride |
| Medium soft | Add $\frac{1}{2}$ tsp chalk $+$ $\frac{1}{2}$ tsp Potassium Chloride |
| Moderately hard | Add 1 tsp calcium chloride |
| Hard | Dilute 25% with rainwater, add $\frac{1}{2}$ tsp calcium chloride |
| Very hard | Dilute 50% with rainwater, add $\frac{1}{2}$ tsp calcium chloride |

'After a vigorous boiling, the water should be allowed to cool to sediment the chalky deposits and the soft water gently racked off and treated as necessary'.

# 9 Let's start brewing

By far the majority of home brewers started off using a beer kit. The advantages of this approach is that no brewing knowledge is necessary and only a few basic pieces of equipment are required.

As your enthusiasm for home brewing grows, so too will your thirst for knowledge and a more professional product. By reading through this book you will know the extra equipment required and so you can play ahead and start acquiring the necessary articles to build your own professional brewery.

Do not keep the fact that you are home brewing a secret, if such a thing was possible! Tell your relatives, friends, and neighbours all about it. Purposely let slip little statements like 'what I really need is an 'old' Burco boiler' (or whatever) and you will be amazed at the response. What's the betting Aunt Euphemia has a Burco in her attic ... now, (wink!) do you get the idea!

## Basic equipment
### Fermentation vessel

Purposely designed fermentation bins are stocked by home brew retailers. A 25 litre size is ideal for brews up to 23 litres (5 gallons) and most types have a snap-on lid, strong carrying handle and a measuring scale on the side. Some types also have a small tap fitted at the base and I would consider this an advantage.

### Air-lock

A gadget fitted to fermentation vessels to vent off the carbon dioxide gas produced during fermentation. The gas escapes through a barrier of water, or preferably sodium metabisulphite, which will prevent bacteria and oxygen from attacking the brew.

## Syphon

A syphon consists of about 2 metres of polyvynal tubing connected to a glass or plastic stem, which allows beer to be drawn off without disturbing the yeast sediment. When brewers use a syphon we always refer to the practice as 'racking'.

## Brewers paddle

These are made from polypropyline with extra long handles for reaching to the depths of bins and barrels. They might be spoon shaped or flat ended with various cut-outs designed to increase Wort agitation. If your choice of draught container has a small sealing cap, then the spoon will require trimming before it can be used for rousing in primings and finings.

## Small funnels

I use two small funnels, one for transferring sterilising solutions from bottle to bottle and the other 'dry' one for adding priming sugar.

## Bottles

Quite a variety of bottles can be used to store home brewed lager, each with some advantages and disadvantages. Read the chapter on bottled beer before investing in a choice.

## Barrels

The home brew trade has produced a fascinating variety of designs in draught containers at a price to suit everyone's pocket. Read through the chapter on draught beer, then nip out to your local retailer and take your pick!

## Hydrometer

The hydrometer is an inexpensive instrument which the beginner will find indispensible for judging when it is safe to bottle or cask his brew. It is easier to use and read if the sample of beer is contained in a trial jar, a tall cylindrical glass or plastic tube.

## Kitchen equipment

A set of scales will be necessary for weighing out ingredients. A set of measuring spoons are a must for accurate dispense of priming sugar and various treatments in brewing. A sieve is handy for straining small amounts of hops and grains. A large saucepan or pressure cooker will be required occasionally. A liquidiser makes light work of crushing the small amounts of coloured malts required and all-purpose cleaning cloths make cleaning and sterilising easier.

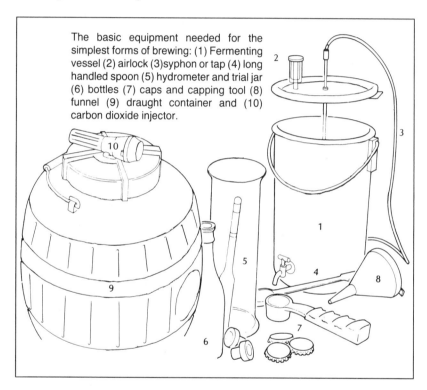

The basic equipment needed for the simplest forms of brewing: (1) Fermenting vessel (2) airlock (3)syphon or tap (4) long handled spoon (5) hydrometer and trial jar (6) bottles (7) caps and capping tool (8) funnel (9) draught container and (10) carbon dioxide injector.

## Your first brew

A bear kit is an excellent base for the beginner to build on and learn a few techniques which can be applied in the production of future brews.

A beer kit wort is made up with $\frac{2}{3}$rds of hopped malt extract and $\frac{1}{3}$rd of added white sugar. In most cases this works out at about 1.8 kg of extract and 1 kg of sugar in 23 litres. The ratio of sugar is more than twice the upper limit used in commercial brewing and the reason for this is to balance the cheapness of sugar against the expensive malt extract and so keep the cost of a kit competitive. Too high a proportion of sugar produces a hard 'tangy' flavour in beer, reduces the palate fullness (body) and head retentions. By making small adjustments to the sugar ratio, the lager will be considerably improved.

## Dealing with sugar

If we take a kit with 1.8 kg of malt extract and 1 kg of sugar, this will produce an original gravity of 1040 in a 23 litre brew. Should we delete the sugar altogether, the lager would be weak and insipid with a gravity of 1024. Therefore, if we are going to delete the sugar we must either replace it with a superior ingredient to maintain the required original gravity, or reduce the volume of the brew to a gravity which will maintain adequate strength.

For example, by deleting 500 g of sugar and reducing the volume to 18 litres, the body and head retention are improved and the strength of the brew remains roughly the same. Should we remove the sugar completely and only brew 13.5 litres, a very full bodied lager will result, with increased hop bitterness and head retention.

If you are not too happy about reducing the volume of your brew (and that is understandable!), then we should look at an alternative to sugar. We have already seen that the quality of a beer improves as the malt to sugar ratio increases, so by swopping 500 g of sugar for 500 g of light dried malt extract, the gravity will be roughly the same but a fuller, although slightly less bitter palate will result. If you feel the bitterness could be a little sharper, try adding Munton & Fisons 'hopped' dried malt extract in the next brew. Yet another approach is to use barley syrup. 500 g of barley syrup will reduce the gravity a little but will greatly improve the palate fullness and head retention without increasing the maltiness of the brew.

Once you have tried out a few brews, you might like to try replacing the remaining 500 g of sugar with glucose chips or powder which will dry-flavour the character of the brew.

## Adjusting bitterness

Lightly hopped lagers, in my view, lack character and can taste somewhat insipid like so many American beers and sadly, like some British ones as well.

The easiest way to increase bitterness is to use 'isomerised' hop extract. As previously explained, the dosage in 'unhopped' wort is about 8 to 10 drops per 5 litres. We can assume therefore that the lager kit contains roughly this amount and so to add the same again, will make the lager twice as bitter. The safest plan is to add slightly less than half the number of drops, say 2 drops per 5 litres, and adjust future amounts to taste. Don't forget to note the number of drops or the accuracy of your experiments will be lost.

Another method is to try the pressure cooking techniques described in chapter 16, or just simmer a cupful of Saaz or Challenger hops in a litre (2 pints) for about 30 minutes and then strain it into the brew.

No doubt by this time you are dying for a pint! So let's start brewing.

# Initial preparation

Open the beer kit and use some of the malt extract to prepare a yeast starter.

Check the equipment you will require and make sure it is clean and sterile.

Before you start preparing the brew, decide on what alterations you are going to make and have the ingredients at hand.

# Brewing

Remove the label from the can and stand it in some hot water to reduce the viscosity of the extract and make it easier to pour. Pour the extract into the fermenting bin and rinse out the dregs in the can with some hot water and add this to the bin as well. Should you decide to use barley syrup, this should be treated likewise. Dried malt extract should be thoroughly dissolved in some hot water before being added to the bin. Glucose chips and powder should be treated likewise.

Add any sugar to be used to the bin. If you are using fresh cone hops to increase bitterness simmer them for 30 minutes before you intend to brew and then strain the hot liquid onto the sugars in the bin.

Stir the wort to ensure all is dissolved and top up the brew to 23 litres with hot and cold water as required to ensure the final volume has a temperature range 15–18C (60–68F). The wort should now taste 'bitter-sweet'.

Once the temperature has stabilised, add the yeast starter, snap on the lid of the bin and allow the brew to ferment for four to five days. Fermentation can be considered to be over when bubbles cease to escape through the air-lock and the lager tastes 'bitter-dry'. It is much safer of course to check this with a hydrometer and the beer can be bottled when the gravity has stabilised below a specific gravity of 1.010.

BL-E

# 10 Cleaning your equipment

Cleaning and sterilizing equipment is an important function and any neglect can quickly ruin a brew. Remember, that bacteria cannot be seen by the naked eye, but they are all around us hiding in every nook and cranny just waiting for the opportunity of a suitable medium in which to flourish. Beer wort and dregs are just that and provide bugs with a nutritious environment and within a short period of becoming infected growths and moulds will quickly start to appear in liquids and on equipment.

Cleaning and sterilizing is not a laborious task and should be undertaken with enthusiasm in the sure knowledge that its function will ensure a healthy brew up and a satisfying pint.

There are a number of cleaning and sterilizing agents available to us.

## Silana pf crystals

This is an excellent cleaner and steriliser originally marketed for general kitchen use. Its effectiveness was quickly recognised by home brewers and we probably use more of it than housewives. The makers claim it removes lipstick like magic, so it should go down a treat with the ever increasing number of lady home brewers! It retails in 454 g packs (lb) and is suitable for cleaning crockery, plastics and glassware.

## Chempro SDP

This is perhaps the most popular cleaner and steriliser used by home brewers. It is also used in commercial brewing and can safely be used to clean all our equipment, including aluminium and stainless steel boilers. It retails in 100 g sachets to make 90 litres or 500 g packs to make 450 litres. Comprehensive instructions for its use are written on the pack.

# Boots

Boots supply as combined cleaner and steriliser in powder and tablet form. The tablets are a convenient method to use and store this effective agent.

# Sodium metabisulphite

This is an effective sterilising agent popular with home brewers. The powder is made up to a strength of 2 teaspoons per litre (1 tsp/Pt) of cold water and its potency can be increased by the addition of a pinch of citric acid. The acid releases the sulphur dioxide, but take care not to inhale the fumes as they are very irritant!

It is very important when using this agent to wet the whole surface of the equipment to ensure it is sterile. Only use a fresh batch for sterilising equipment which will be in contact with the brew. Reserve the used solution for sterilising bins and barrels before they are stored.

# Campden tablets

This is a convenient source of sodium metabisulphite in tablet form. They are a useful anti-oxident when lagering or during the fining process. Each tablet contains some 50 mg/lt of sodium metabisulphite and 2 tablets for 23 litres should be quite adequate.

# Cleaning equipment

Aluminium and stainless steel boilers should be given a thorough scrubbing out with steel wool and a little washing-up liquid. Pay particular attention to the heating element as trace amounts of sugars will caramelise into a hard film in successive brews which will effect the colour and taste in future brews. The tap should be stripped down occasionally and given a good clean with steel wool. Don't forget crevices and areas such as the rim of the lid as this is where the cunning little bugs will lurk just waiting for the chance to attack your tasty brew. When cleaning is finished, boil a few litres in the boiler for about ten minutes with the lid on to steam out any odours from the cleaning process. Run the discarded water out through the tap and give the boiler a final wipe with a dry cloth. Remember too, that the outside of the boiler is as important as the inside.

High density plastic boilers, such as the Bruheat and Electrim Bin, should be given a good clean out with a nylon scouring pad after every brew-up. Again it pays dividends to give the heating element a thorough clean but do this with steel wool and never use sodium metabisulphite to sterilise the boiler or the element will suffer from corrosion.

# Fermentation bins/small gear

Fermentation bins should always be thoroughly cleaned and sterilised before use. However, with repeated use the polythene starts to darken a little as the mildly absorbent plastic soaks up some of the colouring from successive brews. The best way to overcome this is to soak the fermenter in a cleaner and steriliser for about twelve hours or so. When carrying out this task it is a good idea to pitch in small funnels, air-locks, plastic spoons and the syphon. When adding the syphon, suck up the fluid (taking great care not to swallow any of the cleaning fluid!) and then lower the syphon into the bucket ensuring that it is fully immersed. Any other piece of plastic utensils can also be cleaned in this way but under no circumstances add anything with *metal parts.*

# Barrels

Barrels should be cleaned and sterilised before and after use. They too should be given the occasional lengthy soak to remove stains from the inaccessible areas. The tap should be removed and inspected for dirt and damage and soaked in a strong cleaner for a few hours. During operation the tap is the only access point for bacteria and particularly during the warmer months moulds can grow on the dregs that linger there. The tap should therefore be kept scrupulously clean at all times and this is easy to do with a pipe cleaner soaked in sodium metabisulphite. Keep a small jar of steriliser by the barrel and after each session clean out the tap interior with the wetted pipe cleaner.

Should you use a drip cup with your barrel then this too must be cleaned out after each evening's imbibing.

# Glassware

Bottles are easily cleaned by soaking them for a few hours in a Chempro solution. Drain them well after cleaning and give them a final rinse out with sodium metabisulphite to neutralise the effects of Chempro. Hydrometers and trial jars should only require a short soak periodically and the thermometer can be cleaned at the same time. Just fill up the trial jar with a 'cold' Chempro solution and place the instruments in it. After half an hour take them out and turn them upside down for a further half hour. Rinse them with sodium metabisulphite, dry them and store. Don't forget to clean and sterilise your 'starter' bottle as well. Drinking glasses can be cleaned with Chempro or Silana pf crystals which will remove all traces of grease and beer film to leave them sparkling clear and bright. A dry clean 'glass' cloth is handy for keeping glasses well polished.

# 11 The hydrometer

The hydrometer is a precision instrument designed to float vertically in liquids. It has a bulbous weighted end which gives it stability and a graduated scale which relates to the density of wort in relation to the density of water at 20C.

## How it works

Most people know that it is easier to swim in the sea than in fresh water, this is because the salt increases the density of the water and so will support anything which is the same weight or lighter than the weight of the amount of water it is displacing. The dead sea is a good example of this and it has a very high concentration of salt which gives it exceptionally good buoyancy. Because of its density, non-swimmers can lie back and float in it with ease and read Winemaker & Brewer! The hydrometer works on the same principle, but in our case the salt is replaced with sugar.

A home brew hydrometer should have a range from 1.000 to 1.125 which is adequate for a whole range of beer strengths. The weighted end is calibrated so that the hydrometer sinks to and remains at 1.000 when placed in water at 20C. If sugar is added to water, the liquid becomes thicker or more dense, supporting the hydrometer to a greater degree and so more of the calibrated scale will protrude above the surface of the liquid. During fermentation, the yeast will convert the sugar into alcohol and this coupled with the gradual removal of the weight of sugar will thin out (attenuate) the gravity of the wort. Consequently, the hydrometer will sink into the wort a little deeper each day until all the fermentable sugars are used up by the yeast.

# Using the hydrometer

To use the hydrometer, draw off a sample of wort into a trial jar and place it on a level surface. Immerse the hydrometer in the wort and ensure that the scale area is wetted. Gently spin the hydrometer to dislodge any bubbles which might be clinging to it, aiding its buoyancy which will make it float a little higher and give an inaccurate reading. Allow the

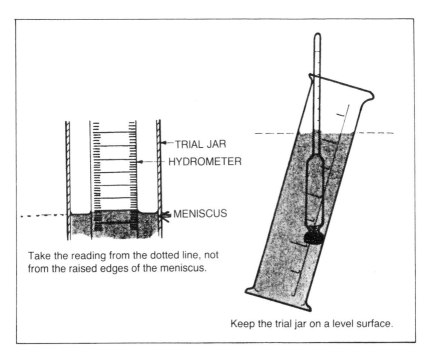

←TRIAL JAR
←HYDROMETER

←MENISCUS

Take the reading from the dotted line, not from the raised edges of the meniscus.

Keep the trial jar on a level surface.

hydrometer to stop spinning and settle in the centre of the jar and check the gravity by taking the reading at the point where the surface of the liquid cuts the stem of the hydrometer. The wort in the trial jar will form a 'meniscus' and will rise up slightly at the edge of the jar and on the stem of the hydrometer. The reading should be taken at eye level.

## Temperature effects

The hydrometer is only accurate at 20C and should the gravity be taken at any other temperature, a false reading will be obtained. For example, if the

63

liquid is warmer than 20C, its volume will be slightly greater due to its expansion and its gravity will be slightly thinner, therefore the hydrometer will sink a little deeper into the wort. Similarly, if the liquid is cooler than 20C, it will contract becoming more dense and so the hydrometer will float a little higher. The readings obtained in such circumstances will not relate accurately to the true density.

All new hydrometers should now be designed to be read at 20C, but a considerable number used by the home brew fraternity will be designed to be read at 60F and so the following correction chart should prove useful.

The following table refers to the corrections to be applied to the indications of hydrometers calibrated at 20C and 60F to give the gravity at 20C.

Hydrometers calibrated at 20C

| Temp C | Correction | Temp F | Correction |
|--------|-----------|--------|-----------|
| 0 | - 2 | 32 | - 2 |
| 5 | - 2 | 40 | - 2 |
| 10 | - 1½ | 50 | - 1½ |
| 15 | - 1 | 60 | - 1 |
| 20 | Correct | 70 | Correct |
| 25 | + 1½ | 80 | + 1½ |

Hydrometers calibrated at 60F

| Temp C | Correction | Temp F | Correction |
|--------|-----------|--------|-----------|
| 0 | - 1½ | 32 | - 1½ |
| 5 | - 1½ | 40 | - 1½ |
| 10 | - 1 | 50 | - 1 |
| 15 | - ½ | 60 | - ½ |
| 20 | + 1 | 70 | + 1 |
| 25 | + 2 | 80 | + 2 |

For example, a wort which indicates a specific gravity of 1.043 on a hydrometer calibrated at 60F, the wort temperature being 25C would have a specific gravity of 1.043 + 2 = 1.45 at 20C.

The hydrometer is also used for checking on the degree of attenuation during fermentation. When taking readings it is not necessary to record the first figure or the decimal point and so a reading of 1.045 is recorded as 45.

## The course of a lager fermentation with an original gravity of 52°

| Time of Pitching | Gravity of Wort degrees | Attenuation in one day | Temp °C |
|---|---|---|---|
| 1 day | 50 | 2 | 7 |
| 2 | 46 | 4 | 8 |
| 3 | 41 | 5 | |
| 4 | 35 | 6 | |
| 5 | 28 | 7 | 10 |
| 6 | 23 | 5 | 12 |
| 7 | 19 | 4 | |
| 8 | 15 | 4 | |
| 9 | 12 | 3 | |
| 10 | 10 | 2 | 6 |
| 11 | 08 | 2 | |
| 12 | 07 | 1 | 4 |

# Calculating strength

The strength of a beer can be simply worked out by recording the 'original' gravity of the wort before the yeast is added and the 'specific' gravity of the beer when the lagering period is over. By subtracting the specific gravity from the original gravity, we can find out how many degrees of sugar the yeast has used up and by dividing the number of degrees by 7.4, we can determine the strength of the brew, thus:

| Original gravity | 1.052 | = 52 |
|---|---|---|
| Specific gravity | 1.007 | = 07 |
| | | |
| Number of degrees | | 45 |

45 degrees divided by 7.4 equals 6% alcohol by volume.

The remaining 7 degrees consist of unfermentable sugars which remain in the lager, giving it body and sweetness to balance the hop bitterness.

# The thermometer

The thermometer partners the hydrometer and is an essential piece of equipment. Although the nation is well established in metrication, many home brewers prefer to work in Imperial measures and so a thermometer with both degrees, centrigrade and fahrenheit, is a good choice. Boots produce a floating thermometer which is handy for taking readings and at the same time leave one free to get on with other brewing matters.

# 12 Degrees of extract

It is important for the home brewer to know the potential yield he can expect from the materials used in brewing. Armed with this knowledge, we have the means of calculating the efficiency of extraction and recovery of extract. Should the home brewer wish to formulate a recipe with a predetermined original gravity, a knowledge of degrees of extract is essential.

The degrees of extract in the following tables are expressed in litre degrees per kilogram (litre°/kg) and pint degrees per pound (pint°/lb). What these values mean, is that when a material has an extract of 296° as it is for lager malt, and if the extract from one kilogram of this is dissolved in water, the total volume of the solution in litres, multiplied by the resulting gravity of the solution in degrees, is equal to 296° at 20C.

For example, if we take the extract from one kilogram of malt dissolved in water and make it up to 23 litres, the resulting gravity would be 12.87 as 23 × 12.87 = 296°.

This makes it easy to check the gravity expected from a brew because the gravity produced by any one constituent is given by the expression:

$$\text{Gravity produced} = \frac{\text{litre° from the ingredient}}{\text{Total volume in litres}}$$

Litre and pint degrees are a very efficient method of calculating extract and are much more accurate than Brewers pounds or gallon degrees.

The simplicity of the system can be best illustrated by working through an example.

67

| | | |
|---|---|---|
| 3 kg lager malt at 296° = | 3 × 296° = | 888° |
| 750 g flaked rice at 323° = | .75 × 323° = | 242° |
| 250 g white sugar at 385° | = .25 × 385° = | 96° |

| | |
|---|---|
| Total expected extract | 1126 Litre° |

The brew was mashed, sparged and boiled up with the hops. The wort recovered in the fermentation vessel measured 25 litres and the gravity at 20C was 1.042. This makes the total extract recovered to be 25 × 42 = 1050 litre°.

The efficiency of recovery is therefore:

$$\text{Gravity produced} = \frac{1050}{1126}, = 93\% \text{ which is quite satisfactory}$$

Many home brewers puzzle over the fact that they do not extract the same values quoted from amateur publications. This is nothing to be alarmed about, as neither do the commercial brewers achieve these values! The values quoted in the table refer to the laboratory extraction rates achieved under ideal conditions and represent the maximum possible extract recovery.

In practice, a somewhat lower value should be expected for a number of reasons. For example, there is always a small amount of unconverted starch left in the grains after mashing which result in a loss of extract. This is one of the reasons why the temperature of the sparge liquor should not exceed 80C (176F) as the starch can be washed out of the grains into the brew where it causes haze.

The spent grains after mashing retain a few degrees of extract which is not recovered by sparging. By sparging with excessive amounts of water, this loss might be recovered, but so too will be the undesirable amounts of polyphenols which makes the lager taste excessively astringent. Malt fats and silica will be washed through, effecting head retention and imparting a harsh taste in the brew. Ideally, sparging should cease when the runnings from the mash tun have a gravity of 1.003/4.

Hops retain extract after boiling and although some of this is recovered by the hop sparge, there is still a loss of some extract.

The quality of the ingredients particularly lager and pale malts, will vary due to the nitrogen content, its moisture level, its age and how well it has been stored. The efficiency of crushing malt is also very important and poorly crushed grains will result in a poor extract recovery. I always buy my malts ready crushed.

The quality of the brewing water is important, particularly if it contains some calcium sulphate. Untreated chalky water will restrict the mash tun conditions resulting in poor extract recovery.

# Formulating a recipe

As regards the use of the extraction values for the formulation of a recipe, we will take an example that the home brewer wishes to brew 23 litres of premium lager with an original gravity of 1.045. A typical grist composition would be as follows:

> 75% lager malt
> 15% flaked maize
> 10% white sugar

The above percentages *'do not'* refer to the weight of the materials, they refer to the relative *'contributions'* they make to the original gravity.

The total volume required is 23 litres with an original gravity of 45. The total gravity from the ingredients therefore is $23 \times 45 = 1035$ litre°.

## Malt

The laboratory extract for lager malt is 296 litre°/kg and the home brewer should expect 93% of this or, $296 \times .93 = 275$ litre°/kg. The contribution from the malt is required to be 75% thus $1035 \times .75 = 776$ litre°/kg.

At 275 litre°/kg, the t of malt required is

$$\frac{776}{275} = 2.82 \, \text{kg}.$$

## Maize

The laboratory extract for flaked maize is 313 litre°/kg and again we should expect 93% of this, or $313 \times .93 = 291$ litre°/kg.

The contribution from the maize is required to be 15% thus $1035 \times .15 = 155$ litre°/kg.

At 291 litre°/kg the amount of maize required is

$$\frac{155}{291} = 0.53 \, \text{kg}$$

# Sugar

The laboratory extract for sugar is 375 litre°/kg and the contribution is $1035 \times .10 = 103$ litre°/kg.

At 375 litre°/kg we will require $\dfrac{103}{375} = 0.27\,kg$

The lager grist will now consist of the following:

|  |  |
|---|---|
| Lager malt | 2.82 kg |
| Flaked maize | 0.53 kg |

And 270 g of white sugar added during the boiling.

## Degrees of extract table

| Ingredients | Lab Litre/kg | 93% | Lab Pint/lb | 93% |
|---|---|---|---|---|
| Lager malt | 296 | 275 | 237 | 220 |
| Pale malt | 296 | 275 | 237 | 220 |
| Wheat malt | 318 | 295 | 254 | 236 |
| Crystal malt | 268 | 249 | 214 | 199 |
| Cara-pils | 268 | 249 | 214 | 199 |
| Chocolate malt | 268 | 249 | 214 | 199 |
| Roast malt | 265 | 246 | 212 | 197 |
| Brewing flour | 325 | 302 | 260 | 214 |
| Flaked rice | 323 | 300 | 258 | 239 |
| Flaked maize | 313 | 291 | 250 | 232 |
| Flaked wheat | 273 | 253 | 223 | 207 |
| Torrified barley | 253 | 235 | 202 | 187 |
| Torrified wheat | 273 | 253 | 218 | 202 |
| Malt extract (liquid) | 303 | 100% | 242 | 100% |
| Malt extract (dried) | 375 | 100% | 300 | 100% |
| Barley syrup | 279 | 100% | 237 | 100% |
| Golden syrup | 360 | 100% | 288 | 100% |
| Glucose chips | 319 | 100% | 255 | 100% |
| Glucose powder (Dextrose monohydrate) | 319 | 100% | 255 | 100% |
| White sugar | 375 | 100% | 300 | 100% |
| Coloured sugar | 365 | 100% | 292 | 100% |

# 13 Brewing with malt extract

Once you have brewed a lager kit and tried out one or two varieties to it, you will no doubt wish to further your brewing knowledge and experience. The next logical step therefore, is to use unhopped malt extract and formulate your own kit!

Malt extract is an easy substance to use and affords the beginner plenty of scope to produce a range of lager styles with the minimum of fuss and bother.

To achieve best results, a large boiler is essential. The Thorne Electrim Bin and Ritchie Bruheat, although a little on the small side are adequate for this method of brewing. I would also advise you to acquire a 'polypin', which is a collapsible polythene cube used commercially for the take-home trade. They are expendable by the trade and most shopkeepers are only too glad to get rid of them. They are also available in home brew shops. The cube is used as a secondary fermentation vessel and also as a fining container. It is also an excellent 'lagering' tank for the refrigeration techniques which will be discussed later in the book.

## The procedure

Light Pilsner at O.G. 1.032

> 2 kg (4.4 lb) light dried malt extract
> 45 g (1.5 oz) Challenger hops
> Lager yeast

Prepare the yeast starter well in advance of brewing day.

Clean and sterilise the equipment.

Treat the brewing water if necessary.

Add 20 litres (35 pints) to the boiler and bring to boiling point. Meanwhile, pre-mix the dried malt extract and any sugar in a separate bucket and thoroughly dissolve it with some hot water from the boiler.

71

Pour the extract into the boiler, stirring well to ensure it is thoroughly mixed.

Add the quota of malts and hops and boil for one hour.

If desired, use an 'aroma' hopping technique before the end of the boil.

Switch off the boiler and allow the hops to sink before straining the wort into the fermenter. Strain the wort as clean as possible, leaving the hops and protein debris behind.

Cool the wort as rapidly as possible to 15C (60F) and adjust the volume to 23 litres (40 pints). Aerate the wort by vigorous stirring, pitch the yeast starter and leave to ferment.

Ferment the brew in a cool place until the specific gravity drops to a quarter of the original gravity and rack into a polypin.

If the beer is to be bottled, add beer finings and allow the beer to rest for 48 hours. During this time the gravity might drop a degree or so and it can safely be bottled when the gravity stabilises below 1.010.

If the brew is for draught, do not add finings at this stage.

Allow a rest of 48 hours and rack into the barrel. Now add the finings and primings.

In both cases, the brew should be left in a warm place for a few days to encourage the conditioning. Finally mature the beer in a cool place until clear.

Here are a few more recipes for you to try.

## Medium Pilsner

23 litres at O.G. 1.041.

| | | |
|---|---|---|
| 2.5 kg | (5.5 lb) | light dried malt extract |
| 125 g | (4 oz) | crushed crystal malt |
| 60 g | (2 oz) | Saaz hops |
| Hop oil to taste | | |
| Lager yeast | | |

## Dortmunder style

23 litres at O.G. 1.044

| | | |
|---|---|---|
| 2.5 kg | (5.5 lbs) | light dried malt extract |
| 225 g | (8 ozs) | light brown dried malt extract |
| 45 g Hallertaur hop | | |
| Lager yeast | | |

## Munich-bier-style

23 litres at O.G. 1.054

2 kg    (4.4 lbs)  light dried malt extract
1 kg    (2.2 lbs)  dark dried malt extract
500 g   (1 lb)     crushed crystal malt
One sachet of Hallertaur pellets
Vierka Munich-Bier yeast
Hop oil

# Liquid extract recipes

Follow the basic procedure for dried malt extract, but stand the cans in hot water for a few moments to make it easier to pour.

It is very important to ensure the viscous malt extract solution is thoroughly dissolved before adding it to the boiler. Failure to do so might result in heavy droplets of the syrup clinging to the heating element which will stubbornly resist stirring, but will burn on the element during boiling and impart a burnt caramel taste in the brew.

## Pilsner I

23 litres at O.G. 1.038

1.5 kg   (3.3 lbs)  light malt extract
1.0 kg   (2.2 lbs)  barley syrup
125 g    (4 ozs)    crushed crystal malt
225 g    (8 ozs)    white sugar
60 g     (2 oz)     Saaz hops
Vierka Lager-Bier yeast

## Pilsner 2

23 litres at O.G. 1.039

3 kg    (6.6 lbs)  Edme DMS
60 g    (2 ozs)    crushed crystal malt
30 g    (1 oz)     Northdown hops
Half a sachet of Hallertaur pellets
Lager yeast

BL–F

## Pilsner 3

20 litres (35 pints) at O.G. 1.0

| | | |
|---|---|---|
| 3 kg | (6.6 lbs) | light malt extract |
| 125 g | (4 ozs) | white sugar |
| 125 g | (4 ozs) | crushed crystal malt |
| 30 g | (1 oz) | Kent Goldings |
| 30 g | (1 oz) | Saaz hops |

Vierka Lager-Bier yeast


## Dortmunder 1

23 litres at O.G. 1.038

| | | |
|---|---|---|
| 1.7 kg | (3.7 lbs) | Boots malt extract |
| 1 kg | (2.2 lbs) | Barley syrup |
| 225 g | (8 ozs) | glucose chips |
| 30 g | (1 oz) | Challenger hops |
| 30 g | (1 oz) | Hallertaur hops |

Lager yeast


## Dortmunder 2

23 litres at O.G. 1.043

| | | |
|---|---|---|
| 3 kg | (6.6 lbs) | Edme SFX |
| 225 g | (8 ozs) | white sugar |
| 75 g | (2.5 ozs) | Saaz hops |

Lager yeast


## Munchener 1

20 litres at O.G. 1.039

| | | |
|---|---|---|
| 2 kg | (4.4 lbs) | Medium malt extract |
| 500 g | (1.0 lb) | crushed crystal malt |
| 125 g | (4 ozs) | crushed chocolate malt |
| 30 g | (1 oz) | Styrion Goldings |
| 30 g | (1 oz) | Saaz for aroma |

Vierka Munich-Bier yeast

# Munchener 2

| | | |
|---|---|---|
| 4 kg | (4.4 lbs) | medium malt extract |
| 500 g | (1 lb) | crushed crystal malt |
| 225 g | (8 ozs) | crushed chocolate malt |
| 125 g | (4 ozs) | black malt |
| 30 g | (1 oz) | Northdown hops |
| 30 g | (1 oz) | Hallertaur for aroma |

Munich-Bier yeast

# 14 Mashing with malt extract

You will recall how I explained in 'How lager is brewed', the various processes used to mash malt and cereals into fermentable sugars. These methods refer to all-cereal mashes designed to deal with various mixtures of grist to produce different styles of beer.

These processes are not necessary with 'diastatic' extract brews, although a short mashing period is necessary to deal with malts and adjuncts in the following recipes which are included to influence flavour and impart subtle nuances in a variety of lager styles.

It is an easy, yet interesting method of brewing and is the half-way stage between the previous straightforward methods of brewing and the more advanced techniques described later.

The diastatic extracts suitable for mashing are:

| | |
|---|---|
| Munton & Fison 'Century' | 100° Lintner |
| Edme 'Super-Flavex' | 80° Lintner |
| Edme 'Diastatic' Malt Syrup | 55° Lintner |

Degrees 'lintner' refer to the strength of the diastase, which in turn can determine the amount of adjuncts which can be successfully mashed. For flavour and practical purposes, adjuncts should be kept below 20%.

Water treatments are not strictly necessary for this type of brewing as only small amounts of grains are used. Chalk however, is best removed by boiling prior to brewing as it interferes with the reaction and brings out a harshness from the ingredients.

Pilsners are particularly prone to problems associated with chalk but Muncheners and Bocks containing acidic roast malts can tolerate moderate chalky water without ill-effects.

The liquor to grist ratio depends very much on the composition of the recipe and the method of mashing employed. Generally, a fluid mash gives good results using about 2 litres per kilogram of malt extract and grain (about 2 pints per pound). This amount will vary and be somewhat condensed when mashing with a pot on a stove or using a pan in the oven and will be a little more fluid when maching with a Bruheat or Electrim Bin.

# Pot on a stove

This method is undoubtedly the easiest method of mashing for the beginner as only small amounts of grains are used. Add the stated amount of water to a large pan and raise the temperature to 60C (140F).

Dilute the malt extract in the liquid and stir well to ensure it is thoroughly dissolved.

Stir in the cereals and make sure they do not clump into little lumps. Any lumps which do form must be broken up otherwise unconverted starch will remain in the brew giving it haze. Raise the temperature to 67C (152F), stirring continuously as you do so. When the temperature has stabilised at 67C replace the pan lid and switch off the heat source.

The heat loss during the next thirty minutes will depend on the type of cooker you have. Electric cookers with a solid metal plate will retain the heat longer than the quick-jeat spiral type. Gas cookers can be controlled to a peep and so it might not require to be switched off. In any case the temperature of the mash should be maintained between 64–67C (147–152F) for a quick and efficient conversion of starch to sugar.

After allowing the mash to stand for thirty minutes or so, check the temperature is between these values and if it is on the low side, gently apply heat to bring it back up to 67C. Don't forget to continually but gently stir the mash as you do so, to prevent the sugars burning on the base of the pan.

# Pan in the oven

Switch the oven on to the 70C setting, and allow to warm up. Meanwhile, prepare the mash as per 'pot on a stove' and when the oven reaches 70C, place the container in the oven and turn off the heat.

Check the mash temperature after thirty minutes and should it be necessary, turn on the heat again to maintain the mashing temperature values. As soon as the oven temperature reaches 70C again, turn off the heat.

Mashing should be successfully completed within one hour but it will be necessary to check if all the starches have been converted to sugar. Failure to carry out this simple test might mean that the brew will be subject to haze.

## Starch test

To test for starch, remove a teaspoon of wort and place it in a small white dish. Add one small drop of 'iodine' to the sample and note its colour. If the iodine keeps its reddish-brown colour then mashing has been successful. Should the iodine turn a bluish-black colour, the conversion is not complete and mashing should be continued.

With the good quality malts and malt extracts which are available to use and provided the mashing temperature parameters are not exceeded, mashing should be complete well within one hour.

A SIMPLE METHOD FOR SPARGING — A SIEVE AND A KETTLE

Once you are satisfied that mashing has been successful, the wort requires to be strained into the boiler. If only small amounts of grains are used a kitchen sieve will be adequate but with larger amounts, say about 1.5 kg (3 lbs), a larger sieve is required. I use a domestic flour sieve, 100 mm high with a nylon mesh base and it has wooden walls, varnished with polyurathene to make them watertight. I secure it into a single unit by fitting it between two pieces of wood which support it over the boiler and add two cross members to prevent the sieve from tilling.

An alternative is to use a small plastic bucket, the base riddled with small holes and jammed into the supporting bracket.

Whichever method you use, tip the grains into the sieve and kettle-sparge with 2 or 3 litres of hot water to recover all the extract. When the kettle-sparge is complete, stir in any sugar or syrups in the recipe and make sure they are thoroughly dissolved. Adjust the volume to the stated amount, add the hops and boil for 60 minutes. The boiling volume stated under each recipe is the maximum quantity recommended for small boilers, but should you own a large Burco, very good results will be achieved by increasing the total volume by at least 25%.

When boiling is complete, strain out the hops and cool to 15C (60F) and adjust the volume if necessary with cold water. Pitch the yeast starter, allow to ferment until the gravity drops to a quarter of the original gravity then rack the brew into the secondary fermenter. Bottle or cask.

# Pilsner 1

23 litres at O.G. 1.041

| | | |
|---|---|---|
| 2.5 kg | (5.5 lbs) | DMS |
| 125 g | (4 ozs) | crushed crystal malt |
| 225 g | (8 ozs) | flaked rice |
| 60 g | (2 ozs) | wheat malt, crushed |
| 225 g | (8 ozs) | white sugar |
| 60 g | (2 ozs) | Challenger hops |
| 30 g | (1 oz) | Hallertaur hops for aroma |
| Lager yeast | | |

| | | |
|---|---|---|
| Mash liquor | 5 litres | ( 9 pints) |
| Sparge liquor | 2 litres | ( 4 pints) |
| Boiling volume | 20 litres | (35 pints) |
| Final volume | 23 litres | (40 pints) |

## Pilsner 2

23 litres at O.G. 1.036

| | | |
|---|---|---|
| 2 kg | (4.4 lbs) | DMS |
| 60 g | (2 ozs) | crushed crystal malt |
| 225 g | (8 ozs) | crushed lager malt |
| 225 g | (8 ozs) | flaked maize |
| 125 g | (4 ozs) | crushed wheat malt |
| 225 g | (8 ozs) | white sugar |

1.5 sachets of Hallertaur hop pellets

Hop oil for aroma
Lager yeast                    Method as per Pils No. 1

## Pilsner 3

23 litres at O.G. 1.045

| | | |
|---|---|---|
| 3 kg | (6.6 lbs) | DMS |
| 225 g | (8 ozs) | flaked rice |
| 225 g | (8 ozs) | crushed wheat malt |
| 75 g | (2.5 ozs) | Saaz hops |
| 30 g | (1 oz) | Saaz hops, pressure-cooked for aroma |

Vierka Lager-bier yeast

| | |
|---|---|
| Mash liquor | 5 litres |
| Sparge liquor | 5 litres |
| Boiling volume | 20 litres |

## Dortmunder 1

23 litres at O.G. 1.051

| | | |
|---|---|---|
| 3 kg | (6.6 lbs) | Superflavex |
| 500 g | (1.0 lb) | crushed lager malt |
| 500 g | (1.0 lb) | flaked maize |
| 30 g | (1 oz) | Hallertaur hops |
| 15 g | (½ oz) | Northdown hops |

| | | |
|---|---|---|
| Mashing liquor | 7 litres | (12 pints) |
| Sparge liquor | 4 litres | ( 8 pints) |
| Boiling volume | 20 litres | (35 pints) |
| Final volume | 23 litres | (40 pints) |

## Dortmunder 2

23 litres at O.G. 1.062

2 kg    (4.4 lbs)   National malt extract
3 kg    (6.6 lbs)   crushed lager malt
225 g   (8 ozs)   crushed crystal malt
125 g   (4 ozs)   wheat flour
30 g    (1 oz)    Styrion goldings
30 g    (1 oz)    Hallertaur hops for aroma
Vierka Lager-bier yeast

| Mash liquor | 10 litres | (17 pints) |
|---|---|---|
| Sparge liquor | 10 litres | (17 pints) |
| Boiling volume | 20 litres | (35 pints) |
| Final volume | 23 litres | (40 pints) |

## Munich style

20 litres at O.G. 1.063

3 kg    (6.6 lbs)   Superflavex
225 g   (8 ozs)   crushed lager malt
500g   (1.0 lb)   crushed crystal malt
125 g   (4 ozs)   crushed chocolate malt
30 g    (1 oz)    crushed roast malt
45 g    (1.5 ozs)   Styrion Goldings
$\frac{1}{8}$th tsp hop oil
Vierka Munich-Bier yeast

| Mash liquor | 4 litres | ( 7 pints) |
|---|---|---|
| Sparge liquor | 7 litres | (12 pints) |
| Boiling volume | 20 litres | (35 pints) |
| Final volume | 20 litres | (35 pints) |

## Bock bier

15 litres at O.G. 1.086

2 kg    (4.4 lbs)   crushed lager malt
2 kg    (4.4 lbs)   dark malt extract (boiling only)
500g   (1.0 lb)   crushed crystal malt
30 g    (1 oz)    Target hops

30 g    (1 oz)    Saaz hops for aroma
Plus a few drops of isomerised hop extract to taste after
fermentation

Mash liquor      5 litres
Sparge liquor    7 litres
Boiling volume  15 litres
Final volume   15 litres

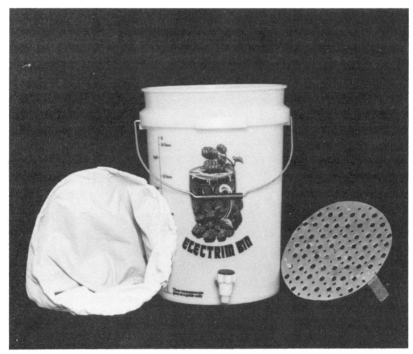

*The Electrim Bin with trivit and grain bag.*

# 15 Decoction mashing

Decoction mashing evolved as a step by step method of dealing with poor quality undermodified malts. The degree of modification will determine the approach to mashing, which will affect the activity of the malt enzymes and the quality of the wort.

The malt enzymes are split into 'proteolytic' and 'diastatic' groups. Both groups operate at different temperatures which splits a decoction mash into 2 distinct phases, although the activity of each phase overlaps each other to some degree. The first stage deals almost exclusively with the degradation of protein and the second phase is essential for the production of sugars.

## The protein rest

The protein rest is necessary to allow the proteolytic enzymes time to degrade the excess protein in undermodified malts so that the resultant brew will be free from haze. However, some protein and polypeptides are necessary in beer as they impart palate fullness and head retention. If proteolysis is prolonged therefore, these substances will be extensively degraded by the enzymes 'protease' and 'peptidase' and so will not be present in sufficient quantities to provide the body and good head retention.

The by products of proteolysis is amino acids which provide the yeast with nutrient for healthy growth.

## First sugar rest

After a period of proteolysis, the mash temperature is raised to 60C (140F) for the first steep or rest. At this temperature, peptidase is destroyed, protease survives but its action is very unstable. The starch begins to solubilise and the diastase starts to convert into sugars.

# Final sugar rest

After a brief rest at 60C, the temperature is boosted to 65C (150F). At this temperature protease is destroyed, the starch is fully solubilised and converted into sugars by the diastase.

'Diastase' is a term used to collectively describe 'all' the enzymes which convert starch to sugars during mashing. The principal enzymes are 'alpha amylase' and 'beta amylase', although 'maltase' and 'dextrinase' are also active.

DECOCTION MASHING

THE ENZYMES ARE PROGRESSIVELY DESTROYED AS MASH TEMPERATURE RISES

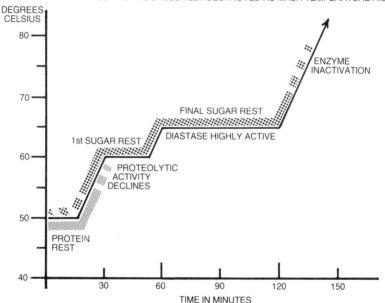

Alpha amylase reduces starch mostly to dextrins, plus a little maltose and glucose. Its action is not however, stable at 65C and although it can tolerate higher temperatures than beta amylase, it dies off within two hours. Its action is more stable in thick mashes, particularly if calcium sulphate is present in the mashing water.

Beta amylase reduces starch and dextrins to maltose. It cannot however, withstand high mash temperatures of 65C and its activity becomes very unstable and is destroyed within one hour.

# pH

The acidity of the mash has important consequences for the efficiency of mashing. Each enzyme has its own pH 'optima' and so in order to satisfy a range of mash tun conditions, some compromises have to be made. For example, alpha amylase works best at pH 5.6 and beta amylase at pH 4.7. Proteolysis is more complete between pH 4.5 and 5.0, and the overall decoction mash efficiency is achieved at pH 5.6. Collectively, the enzymes work best at pH 5.3.

Precise pH control is difficult for the amateur and so a pH colour reading on narrow range pH indicator paper, of 5.0 to 5.5 should be looked for. The guidelines on water treatment should produce this value.

# Mash tun conditions

The conditions set within the mash tun will have a considerable influence on the composition of the wort.

In the production of Pilsners, a fairly fluid mash is best with a liquor/grist ratio of 2.5 litres/kg (2.5 pints/lb). A dilute mash allows the enzymes greater freedom to dissipate throughout the mash and although their activity is unstable, the reactions are speeded up and are best suited to producing maltose. This produces a wort with good attenuation which helps 'dry' flavour a lager.

A fluid mash held at low temperatures for a very long time will encourage excessive proteolysis, resulting in a lack of palate fullness and head retention. Mashes therefore, should not be left to stand overnight.

A limited decoction mash of $1\frac{1}{2}$ to 2 hours should produce a balanced time with roughly 80% maltose and 20% unfermentables which will provide body and good head retention.

A thick mash on the other hand restricts enzyme activity somewhat, due to the insulating effect of the sugars produced. A stiff mash held for short periods at high temperatures, produces a highly dextrinous wort which will lack adequate attenuation and produce an unbalanced beer.

Stiff mashes are best suited for Munchener and Bock styles of beer, with a liquor/grist ratio of about 2 litres/kg (2 pints/lb). As clarity is not a vital element in dark lagers and because such beers are served at cellar temperature (14–15C), a protein rest is not essential. However, a short rest at 60C (140F) for a brief period will favour the action of beta amylase in producing maltose. A final mash temperature between 65C and 68C (150F and 154F) held for one hour should produce a balanced wort with adequate residual sugars which will provide the malty sweetness expected in dark lagers.

# Compromises!

The above liquor/grist ratios work well for brewers who use a large boiler, as the considerable volume of wort collected during mashing and sparging can be boiled off to reduce the volume to the required gravity. With small boilers such as the Bruheat/Electrim Bin, some compromises have to be made. These can either be, to reduce the volume of the sparging liquor and sacrifice a loss of extract. We can consider reducing the amount of liquor to 2 litres per kilogram and mash for two to three hours at just below 65C, which will ensure a wort of good attenuation and maintain the 'dry' characteristic in the brew. The third option is to substitute a portion of the malt content in the grist and replace with malt extract or barley syrup in the boiler. Should you do this, it is important to reduce an equal amount of any adjunct in the grist to avoid overloading the diastase. The flavour of the lager too, will vary somewhat from my original intentions.

# Sparging

It is usual after decoction mashing to boost the temperature of the mash to 75C (167F) to halt enzyme activity. This is not necessary in home brewing and we can halt enzyme activity by commencing sparging.

Sparging is a method of spraying the mash with hot water to rinse out the extract retained by the grains after the wort has been drained and collected in the boiler.

The temperature of the sparge liquor should be about 77C to 80C (170F to 176F). This will reduce the viscosity of the residual sugars and allow them to be freely washed out of the redundant grains. The temperature must not be allowed to rise above 80C or unconverted starch will be leached out and cause haze in the brew.

It is important also that the sparge liquor should have the same composition as the mashing liquor, otherwise, the pH of the grains will alter and encourage the extraction of undesirable substances. The volume of the sparge liquor should be just sufficient to extract the maximum amount of sugars from the grains. Over zealous sparging can result in excessive amounts of polyphenols being extracted which is the principle chill-haze factor in lager and will also affect a bitter astringent flavour.

Silicates from the grain husks and malt fats will also be extracted, producing harsh flavours and a lack of head retention.

Ideally, sparging should cease when the runnings from the mash tun have a gravity of about 1.003/4.

# Practical mashing and sparging

The Bruheat and Electrim Bin have very sensitive thermostats which makes them ideal for close temperature control. A grain bag is necessary to hold the grain above the heating element to prevent charring of the grains.

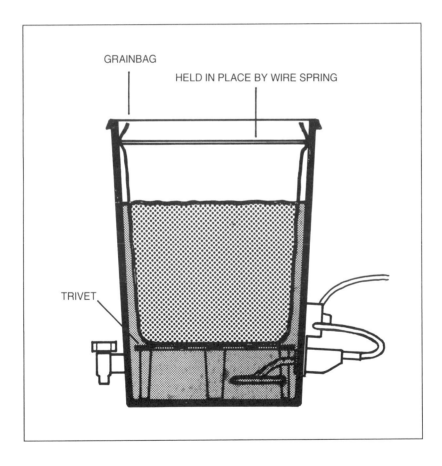

GRAINBAG

HELD IN PLACE BY WIRE SPRING

TRIVET

It is normally recommended that the grain bag is secured by over-lapping it over the top of the boiler and tying it with a drawcord. This means that the bottom of the grain bag is almost half way up the boiler and so the liquor/grist ratio will be far too fluid for an efficient extraction of sugars. To overcome this problem a 'trivet' should be made to support the grain bag just above the heating element. I cut a disc from sheet aluminium 265 mm in diameter to fit my Electrim Bin. The disc was gridded into 25 mm squares and each 'cross' was bored with a 12 mm drill. The centre of each square was bored with a 6 mm drill and the overall effect was a stable platform with good drainage. The trivet is supported on three legs cut from small strips of aluminium, 25 mm × 80 mm. One end of the strips should be bent over and drilled so that it can be secured to the base by a pot rivet. The other end should be filed to slightly round off the edges so there are no sharp edges to damage the bucket.

As the grain bag is resting almost at the bottom of the boiler, it is not long enough to fit over the top and consequently it has a tendency to fall into the boiler when mixing the mash. This small problem is easily overcome by replacing the drawcord with a wire spring made from an aluminium coathanger. Carefully undo the coathanger and straighten it out, feed it through the draw cord seam and join the ends together by twisting them. Make sure the bag is fully stretched before you secure the wire. The bag then sits quite firmly inside the boiler.

## Brewing 'Vogalsang pils'

23 litres at O.G. 1.052

| | | |
|---|---|---|
| Lager malt, crushed | 3.6 kg | (8 lbs) |
| Crystal malt, crushed | 125 g | (4 ozs) |
| Wheat malt, crushed | 125 g | (4 ozs) |
| Flaked maize | 500 g | (1 lb) |
| 'Copper' hops, Hallertaur | 60 g | (2 ozs) |
| 'Aroma' hops, Saaz | 30 g | (1 oz) |
| Yeast, Vierka lager-bier | | |

Ensure that the boiler tap is closed, place in the trivet, grains bag and add 11 litres of soft water, switch the boiler on and allow the temperature to rise to 60C (140F).

Meanwhile, pre-mix the grist in a separate container to ensure an even distribution of non-diastatic material throughout the grain. When the water temperature reaches 60C, stir in the grist in small amounts ensuring that no dry lumps of clogged grain form, otherwise an incomplete conversion will result. When mixing is complete, the temperature should be about 50C (122F).

Set the thermostat to number 2 and allow the mash to stand for fifteen minutes. After the first rest, draw off about 2 litres (4 pints) of wort in a saucepan, raise its temperature to 65C (150F) and return it to the mash. Continue this practice until the mash temperature reaches 60C. This should take about four saucepans and about 10–15 minutes. Allow the mash to rest for fifteen minutes.

Finally, repeat the above procedure to bring the temperature to 65C, set the thermostat to number 3 and mash for a further 1 to 1½ hours.

# Sparging

When mashing is complete, switch off the boiler and place it securely on a kitchen stool so that the tap is just above the collecting vessel.

Open the boiler tap, allow the wort to drain gently from the mash and as soon as the surface of the mash is free of water, sparging should commence.

The easiest way to sparge the mash is to simply 'jug' on the hot water, but do take care to ensure that the whole area of the grains receive an equal amount of water. Most home brewers, however, prefer to use a container fitted with a spray attachment so that more control and a better extraction rate are achieved.

As lager malts are more finely ground than ale malts, they are not so buoyant in the mash tun and so care should be taken when running off the first few litres to ensure the grains do not compact hard down into the small mesh bottom of the grain bag. If this does happen, the mash will be very slow to sparge.

Should you be boiling in a Bruheat/Elecrim Bin, use 12 litres of sparge water but should you use a large Burco, this should be increased to 16 litres.

# Boiling

Boil the wort with the Hallertaur hops for 75 minutes. Select an aroma technique for the Saaz hops and finely strain and cool the wort.

Ferment the wort as previously instructed and bottle or barrel. By noting the original gravity of this brew, you should appreciate that it packs quite a punch, so don't get caught taking an overdose of Pils!

BL–G

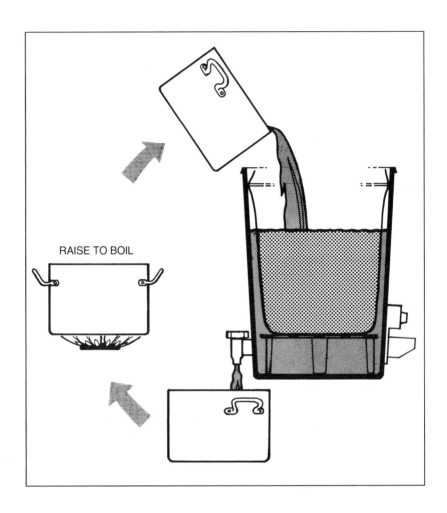

RAISE TO BOIL

# Pilsners
## Sommerbier

23 litres at O.G. 1.033/35

| | | |
|---|---|---|
| 2.5 kg | (5.5 lbs) | crushed lager malt |
| 250 g | (8 ozs) | flaked rice |
| 125 g | (4 ozs) | crushed crystal malt |
| 125 g | (4 ozs) | crushed wheat malt |
| 60 g | (2 ozs) | Challenger hops |

30 g   (1 oz)       Saaz hops (aroma)
Vierka lager-bier yeast
Soft to medium soft water

Mash with 8 litres at 55C for 20 minutes and then boost the temperature to 60C and rest for 15. Finally, raise the temperature to 65C and mash for one hour. Sparge with 11 litres of water at 75C to collect about 18 litres of wort. Adjust the volume to 21 litres and boil for 75 minutes topping up to the 21 litres mark with kettlefulls of boiling water as required. And the challenger hops at the beginning of the boiling and select an aroma technique for the Saaz hops.

When fermentation and lagering are over the final gravity should be about 1.005/7.

## Friockheim brau

23 litres at O.G. 1.039/41

3.0 kg   (6.6 lb)     crushed lager malt
250 g   (8 ozs)     Golden syrup (boiling)
125 g   (4 ozs)     crushed wheat malt
 60 g   (2 ozs)     crushed crystal malt
 90 g   Saaz hops
Glenbrau Danish yeast
Soft water

Follow the procedure for Sommerbier but add the golden syrup with the hop pellets during the boiling. Treat the brew after fermentation with a few drops of hop oil for aroma.

## Broughty brau

23 litres at O.G. 1.036/38

2.5 kg   (5.5 lbs) crushed lager malt
350 g   (12 ozs) flaked maize
 60 g   (2 ozs)    crushed crystal malt
250 g   (8 ozs)    white sugar
1.5 Sachet Hallertaur hop pellets
Glenbrace Danish yeast
Soft water

Follow the procedure for Sommerbrau, adding the sugar to the copper.                                                                                  91

# Dortmunders
## Rosenmuntag bier
23 litres at O.G. 1.047/51

| | | |
|---|---|---|
| 3 kg | (6.6 lbs) | crushed lager malt |
| 500 g | (1.0 lb) | flaked maize |
| 250 g | (8 ozs) | crushed wheat malt |
| 185 g | (6 ozs) | crushed crystal malt |
| 250 g | (8 ozs) | glucose powder |
| 60 g | (2 ozs) | Hallertaur cone hops |

Hop oil for aroma
Vierka lager-bier yeast
Medium soft to moderately hard water

Mash with 11 litres at 55C for 15 minutes and then bring the temperature up to 60C and rest for 15 minutes. Finally, boost the temperature to 65C and mash for one hour. Sparge with 14 litres at 75C to collect about 25 litres of wort. Boil with the hops and glucose for 75 minutes and then cool rapidly to 15C. Adjust the volume to 23 litres, pitch the yeast and ferment in a cold place until the gravity drops to about 1.012 and allow to finish off in a polypin or other sealed container. The bottling gravity should be about 1.008.


## Der Schützenfest bier
23 litres at O.G. 1.043/45

| | | |
|---|---|---|
| 3.6 kg | (8.0 lbs) | crushed lager malt |
| 185 g | (6 ozs) | crushed crystal malt |
| 125 g | (4 ozs) | crushed wheat malt |
| 90 g | (3 ozs) | Saaz cone hops |

A couple of drops of hop oil for aroma
Vierka lager-bier yeast
Moderately hard water

Mash in 10 litres of water at 55C for 20 minutes. Raise the mash heat to 60C and hold for 15 minutes and then boost the temperature to 65C and mash for one hour.

Sparge with 13 litres to collect about 23 litres of wort. Boil with the hops for a full 75 minutes and then strain and cool the wort to 15C and pitch the yeast. Complete the fermentation in a closed container fitted with an air-lock and bottle when the gravity stabilises below 1.010.

# Muncheners
## Schwarz katze bier
23 litres at O.G. 1.043/45

3 kg    (6.6 lbs)    crushed lager
500 g    (1.0 lb)    crushed crystal malt
250 g    (8 ozs)    crushed chocolate malt
125 g    (4 ozs)    crushed black malt
60 g    (2 ozs)    Northdown hops
30 g    (1 oz)    Hallertaur hops (aroma)
Vierka Munich-bier yeast
Moderately hard water

Mash with 8 litres of water at 60C for 15 minutes. Boost to 65C and mash for one hour. Sparge with 12 litres of water at 75C to collect about 20 litres of wort. Add the Northdown hops and boil vigorously for one hour, topping up with boiling water to the 20 litre mark. Cool rapidly to 15C and adjust the volume to 23 litres. Add the yeast and rack into the secondary fermenter when the gravity drops to 1.015 and ferment out. The bottling gravity should be about 1.010.

## Schwarz Schwann bier
20 litres at O.G. 1.046/49

3.0 kg    (6.6 lbs)    crushed lager malt
1.0 kg    (2.2 lbs)    crushed crystal malt
250 g    (8 ozs)    crushed black malt
45 g    (1.5 ozs)    Styrion Goldings
30 g    (1 oz)    Kent Goldings (aroma)
Munich-bier yeast
Moderately hard water

Mash with 9.5 litres of water at 60C for 15 minutes. Raise the temperature to 65C and mash for a further hour. Sparge with 13 litres at 75C to collect about 22 litres of wort. Adjust the volume to 25 litres and boil with the Styrion Goldings for one hour. Cool to 15C and top up to 23 litres. Pitch the yeast and ferment as for Swarzt Katz.

# Spezial biers
## Karlsbrau

23 litres at O.G. 1.076/80

| | | |
|---|---|---|
| 4.5 kg | (9.9 lbs) | crushed lager malt |
| 1.0 kg | (2.2 lbs) | flaked rice |
| 250 g | (8 ozs) | white sugar |
| 250 g | (8 ozs) | crushed crystal malt |
| 110 g | (4 ozs) | Hallertaur hops |
| 30 g | (1 oz) | Saaz for aroma |

Vierka lager-bier yeast
Moderately soft water

Mash the grist in 13 litres of water at 50C for 15 minutes.

Raise the temperature to 60C and rest for 15 minutes. Boost to 65C and mash for 1 hour.

Sparge with 15 litres to collect about 28 litres of wort.

Add the Hallertaur hops and boil for 75 minutes. Choose an aroma technique for the Saaz hops.

Finally mature the brew for six to eight weeks.

## Kiaserbrau

20 litres at O.G. 1.075/79

| | | |
|---|---|---|
| 4 kg | (8.8 lbs) | crushed lager malt |
| 750 g | (1.5 lbs) | flaked maize |
| 500 g | (1.0 lb) | white sugar |
| 250 g | (8 ozs) | crushed crystal malt |

1.5 Dachets Hallertaur pellets
30 g (1 oz) Golding hops  boiling
Hop oil for aroma
Vierka lager-bier yeast
Moderately soft water

Follow the procedure for Karlsbrau, but mash with 12 litres of water and sparge with 13 litres to collect about 25 litres of wort.

## Vienna style

23 litres at O.G. 1.044/47

3.5 kg    (7.7 lbs)   crushed lager malt
300 g     (10 ozs)    crushed crystal malt
250 g     (8 ozs)     crushed wheat malt
45 g      (1.5 ozs)   Styrion Goldings
Vierka Munich-bier yeast

This is a richly flavoured amber coloured lager type, with a light hop character.

Mash in 10 litres of moderately soft to moderately hard water. Allow a short rest at 60C for about 15 minutes and then boost the temperature to 65C and mash for 1 hour.

Sparge with 15 litres of water at 75C to collect 25 litres of wort. Boil with the hops for 75 minutes and adjust the volume to 23 litres.

Mature for 4 weeks.


## Weizen bier

20 litres at O.G. 1.041

2 kg      (4.4 lbs)   crushed wheat malt
500 g     (1.0 lb)    crushed lager malt
30 g      (1 oz)      crushed crystal malt
250 g     (8 ozs)     glucose powder
45 g      (1.5 ozs)   Hallertaur cone hops
A hint of hop oil for aroma
Top fermenting beer yeast
Moderately hard water

A 'hybrid' style of lager fermented with a top yeast and lagered for about 4 weeks. It has a pleasant clean sharp taste and makes a good thirst quencher when served with a slice of lemon.

Mash in 12 litres of water at 50C for 20 minutes. Boost the temperature to 60C and hold for 20 minutes, finally raise the temperature to 65C and mash for 1 hour and 20 minutes.

Sparge with 13 litres of hot water at 75C to collect about 25 litres. Boil for one hour to reduce the volume to just over 20 litres and cool to 15C. Pitch the 'top' yeast and ferment until the gravity drops to 1.010 and rack into a polypin. Allow the brew to ferment out and then add beer finings. Rack into a pressure barrel and treat with krausen wort and after a few days in a warm place finally mature at 10C if possible for 4 weeks. The use of a refrigerator would be an advantage with this brew.

# Bock bier
## Bavarian maid
20 litres at O.G. 1.051/56

| | | |
|---|---|---|
| 2.5 kg | (5.5 lbs) | crushed lager malt |
| 1.0 kg | (2.2 lbs) | crushed crystal malt |
| 125 g | (4 ozs) | crushed black malt |
| 125 g | (4 ozs) | crushed chocolate malt |
| 500 g | (1.0 lb) | dark liquid malt extract (boiling) |
| 60 g | (2 ozs) | Northdown hops |
| 30 g | (1 oz) | Styrion Goldings |

Munich-bier yeast
Soft to moderately hard water

Mash in 7 litres of water at 60C for 15 minutes. Raise the temperature to 65C and mash for a further one hour. Sparge with 14 litres at 75C to collect just over 20 litres. Boil with the hops vigorously for 60 minutes, topping up with boiling water if necessary. Cool the wort to 15C, pitch the yeast and ferment until the gravity drops to 1.022 and rack into 4 × 4.5 litre winemaking jars and allow to ferment out under the protection of an air-lock. It is preferable to bottle this brew and mature it for at least 4 to 6 weeks.

## Dopplebock
10 litres at O.G. 1.098/103

| | | |
|---|---|---|
| 1.5 kg | (3.3 lbs) | crushed lager malt |
| 500 g | (1.0 lb) | crushed crystal malt |
| 250 g | (8 ozs) | crushed chocolate malt |
| 1.0 kg | (2.2 lbs) | dark liquid malt extract (boiling) |

75 g Target cone hops/Northdown hops
2 small drops of hop oil
Moderately hard water
$\frac{1}{2}$ teaspoon Vierka Munich-bier yeast

*Sparging with the Electrim Bin.*

97

Mash in 5.5 litres of water at 60C for 15 minutes. Boost to 65C and mash for a further hour. Sparge with 10 litres at 75C to collect about 15 litres of wort. Boil with the malt extract and cone hops until the volume is reduced to just over 10 litres. Cool rapidly to 15C and ferment until the gravity drops to 1.025 and rack into 2 × 4.5 litre winemakers jars and ferment out under an air-lock. The bottling gravity should stabilise at about 1.020/22.

# 16 Boiling the wort

The consequences of wort boiling are:

It sterilises the wort.

Changes 'sweet wort' into 'bitter wort' as the alpha acids from the hop resins are extracted and converted into soluble and bitter iso-alpha acids which give beer its pleasant bitter tang.

Destroys the enzymes active during mashing but not required during the later stages of brewing, where their continued activity will upset the balance of sugars produced in the mash tun.

Extracts tannins from the petals and strig of the hops which will assist the coagulation and precipitation of wort protein.

Condenses the wort.

Causes slight caramelisation of wort sugars.

Purges the aromatic essential oils of hops to the atmosphere.

## Suitable boilers

Domestic culinary boilers, as supplied to the catering trade are available in sizes from 15 to 18 litres (26 to 31 pints). Some are fitted with taps which is an advantage.

The Thorn 'Electrim Bin' and Richie Products 'Bruheat' are excellent little boilers of about 25 litres capacity (43 pints). They are made from polypropylene and can withstand repeated use up to 130C (226F). Because their capacity is limited to 25 litres, the initial boiling volume should be restricted to 21 litres to allow adequate space for the initial violent turbulance of the boiling. When the boil quietens down a bit, the volume can be increased a little by topping up with kettles of boiling water which will prevent the wort from becoming too condensed.

They are ideal for malt extract brewing but a little on the small side for coping with the large amounts of collected wort from an all grain mash. When brewing such recipes, it is important that the whole wort is boiled to secure clarity in the final beer and consequently this means two boilings.

Burco boilers of 5, 7, 5 and 10 gallons are excellent, particularly the large sizes, as they can cope with large volumes of wort. The older types which you can still acquire should have the following serial numbers (761, 765, 750, 300, 305, and the modified 375) which will ensure that no toxic materials are present in their construction.

The modern stainless steel Burco has a capacity of 27 litres (47 pints) and although a little expensive it will make a good investment for the serious home brewer.

# Boiling

The size of the boiler can effect the character of the final beer. In a small boiler, all the ingredients are condensed which results in less hop bitterness being extracted and the wort sugars becoming too caramelised which might produce too heavy a palate in delicate Pilsners. A Munchener on the other hand will benefit from a condensed boil as the maltiness of the brew is increased.

Optimum hop bitterness is achieved with a full 90 minutes boiling but because malt extract has previously been boiled, this length of boiling might precipitate too much of the foam forming material.

Fortunately, adequate hop bitterness and character are extracted in a 60 minute boiling with the advantage of improved head retention. All-grain worts are a different matter and for really first class results, the wort should be diluted in excess of the final volume and condensed during a vigorous boiling of at least 75 minutes.

Better bitterness from the hops is achieved in a dilute wort and clarity in the final beer is assured with this length of boiling. The acquisition of a large Burco boiler is a real boon to the all-grain brewer as they can deal with large volumes of wort. Should you already have one, then the volumes for the malt extract recipes can be increased by about 25%.

The effects of boiling is the same for all types of boilers, with considerable surface activity which increases if the lid of the boiler is replaced completely. Should you do this, the hops will bloat up and boil over the rim of the boiler in a heaving sticky frothing mass. It is wise, therefore, to only half cover the boiler with the lid until the initial surface activity quietens down then it can be covered a little more to encourage a good rolling boil. The lid should not however be replaced completely or the same boil-over effects will result.

When boiling with the Bruheat or Electrim Bin, a full vigorous boiling is best without the lid being snapped on. Should you fit the lid however, the control dial should be set to allow a quieter boiling but with some agitation and this should be achieved on a setting of 7–8.

When these boilers are simmering vigorously at these settings, there is a considerable jet of steam escaping from the vent hole on the lid and it is important that the vent does not become blocked. Take care also not to accidentally scald yourself and have the boiler well out of the way of children.

Many home brewers boil their worts outside the home so that the neighbours can enjoy the delightful fragrance of hops! Boiling worts outside in Summer presents no problems, but come the Winter, and the chill factor, particularly if a wind is blowing which can be considerable, small boilers can struggle to maintain boiling temperatures. To overcome this, I wrap my boiler in a hot water cylinder jacket. Only the wall of the boiler should be covered and the top left free for the steam to escape and to make inspection easier. A cheap and effective 'duvet' can be made for your boiler by cutting an old blanket to fit around the boiler and twice its height. Double it over, crudely stitch it to make a large pocket and stuff it with glass wool used for insulating lofts.

# Hopping
## Cone hops

To encourage maximum bitterness out of the hops, they should be added at the beginning of the boiling. Do this as soon as the heating element is covered with wort and as sparging commences, the wort will gently simmer away under a blanket of hops. It is important too with malt extract brews to add them at the start, otherwise you risk the danger of the wort boiling over and perhaps causing an accident. As hops lower the surface tension of worts, the problem is reduced. The other advantage is that the hops are given time to soak before the boiler is full and this too helps to reduce the bloating effect during boiling.

The hop cones should be added loose so that they freely flocculate throughout the wort, increasing the agitation which assists the separation of protein. This is obviously less important with malt extract brews but because the extraction of hop resin is restricted somewhat with cone hops, we should do everything possible to encourage the maximum bitterness out of the resins. Cone hops provide a natural filter bed through which to strain the cloudy wort when boiling is complete.

## Pelleted hops

Pellets and powders should be boiled as for cone hops. They provide a little tannin but do not contribute any bulk to the wort and so the value of wort agitation is lost. This does not mean however, that your worts will not clear bright, but it is a point to bear in mind and ensure that worts are boiled as vigorously as possible.

Because pellets disintegrate during boiling, the wort should be strained through a piece of muslin to strain out the wort debris.

On the credit side, pellets and powders are more fully utilised during boiling than cone hops and a better bitterness is achieved. I rarely use pellets on their own, however, and achieve good results when they are blended with cone hops which filter my worts bright.

## Hop 'Copper' extracts

These can be used to partially or completely replace cone and pelleted hops. Their bitterness is fully utilised during boiling, although I find it best to use it as part of a hop blend. The complete replacement dose is about 15 ml per 5 litres ($\frac{1}{2}$ fluid oz/gal).

## Aroma techniques

The essential oils of hops are very volatile and are almost totally evaporated during a long boiling. To compensate for this, brewers employ a variety of 'late' hopping methods.

## Late hopping

This is a very common approach used to impregnate the brew with the aromatic oils. About 10 minutes from the end of boiling, a quantity of hops possessing a good aroma are stirred into the wort and the ensuing boiling extracts the oils. A small amount of the oils are lost by this method but sufficient are retained in the wort to give it a light and pleasant aroma.

# Hot soaking

This method in my view is a much better approach. A quantity of hops are stirred into the brew when the boiling is finished. The lid of the boiler is replaced and the temperature dial just set to allow sufficient heat which will produce thermal currents which will flocculate the cones throughout the wort without producing any significant evaporation. This should continue for about 10–15 minutes with a further 20 minutes soak after the heat is switched off. This further rest will also give the hops and protein debris time to sink to the bottom of the boiler.

# Pressure cooked hops

This is by far the best method which I have used. The aroma is fresh and hoppy and results are first class every time.

Add hops to cold water using a ratio of one litre to 30g of hops. Allow the hops to soak a while and become a little soggy, bring the cooker to one Bar pressure (15psi) and hold for 5 minutes, switch off the heat source, allow the cooker to cool naturally to atmospheric pressure and then add all the contents to the main boiler. Allow a 20 minute soak in the boiler before straining off the wort.

# Straining hops

It is desirable that the bitter wort is run off as clear as possible with a minimum amount of protein in suspension. An excellent 'hop back', or strainer, can be made from a piece of expanded aluminium type 351A as supplied by the Expanded Aluminium Company. The aluminium should be cut so that it fits tightly inside the boiler and should be supported on 3 legs so that it sits just about tap level. The small diamond shaped openings allow a full and vigorous boiling but hold back the cone hops which act as a very effective filter.

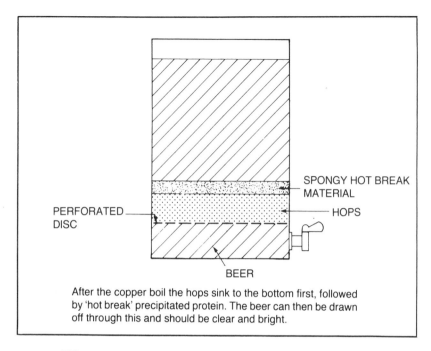

SPONGY HOT BREAK MATERIAL

HOPS

PERFORATED DISC

BEER

After the copper boil the hops sink to the bottom first, followed by 'hot break' precipitated protein. The beer can then be drawn off through this and should be clear and bright.

## Hop sparge

It is necessary to sparge the spent hops in the boiler after straining is completed as they retain a considerable amount of fermentable extract. The runnings from the hops sparge will inevitably contain a considerable amount of wort protein debris and it is important that this is not washed through into the clean wort. It should therefore be collected in a separate container and the solids allowed to sediment before gently racking off the clear wort. Use about 1.5 litres (3 pints) of hot water for sparging.

## Adding sugar

All 'copper' sugars are best pre-dissolved in a bucket using some of the hot wort from the boiler.

## Irish Moss

This is a 'copper' clarifying agent produced from Carragheen Moss, a type of seaweed which is dried and coursely ground before it is used in brewing.

Irish moss carries a 'negative' charge which reacts with the 'positive' charge of the complex wort proteins, this ensures a good 'break' or separation of protein from the wort during boiling and subsequently good clarity in the finished beer.

To achieve good results, one teaspoon should be added about 20–30 minutes from the end of the boiling. It should not be added any earlier or its effectiveness will be reduced by the degrading effects of the hot wort.

# The hot break

The 'hot' break is a term used to describe the phenomena met during boiling when the protein substances separate from the wort. The 'break' looks like little grey flocks finely dispersed throughout the liquid which sediment with the hops when boiling ceases. When the wort is strained off, the break retained by the hops has a scum-like appearance.

The break is encouraged by a vigorous and agitated boiling, particularly if some calcium sulphate or chloride is included in the water treatment. Carbonate water tends to restrict the break and so it is important to remove as much of it as possible before brewing pale Pilsners.

*A simple but effective hop strainer made from expanded aluminium.*

Long boilings precipitate a considerable amount of break which also contains some foam stabilising products, and so a balance must be struck between clarity and head retention. Generally with all-grain worts, both criteria are met with a 75 minute boiling. Should beers produced from malt extract show persistently poor head retention, the boiling should be split into two. Boil the hops initially in 15 litres or so of water for about 45 minutes, and then add the malt extract for the remaining 16–20 minutes of the boiling.

# 17 Cooling the wort

Rapid cooling of wort is deemed essential for the following reasons:

To achieve the 'cold' break.

To aerate worts.

To rapidly lower the temperature so that yeast can be pitched and reduce the chances of bacteria attacking the brew.

## The cold break

The cold break is achieved as the temperature falls below 50C (144F), and at this temperature a fine mist-like material precipitates from the wort. Should the break material be considerable, then it should be removed to prevent problems later in the brewing process. The small amounts from malt extract brews should not present any problems.

## Aeration

Should your fermenter be fitted with a tap, an excellent way to aerate the wort is to place it on a kitchen stool, or better still on a worktop and run the wort into another container. The splashing is considerable at first but it soon quietens down and effective aeration is achieved. There is usually no further need for aeration during fermentation.

Another method is to simply pour the wort from one container to another or vigorously stir the wort with a brewer's paddle.

## Methods of cooling

Rapid cooling of worts for most home brewers usually means standing the container of hot wort in a bath of cold water or leaving it outside on the doorstep during Winter months.

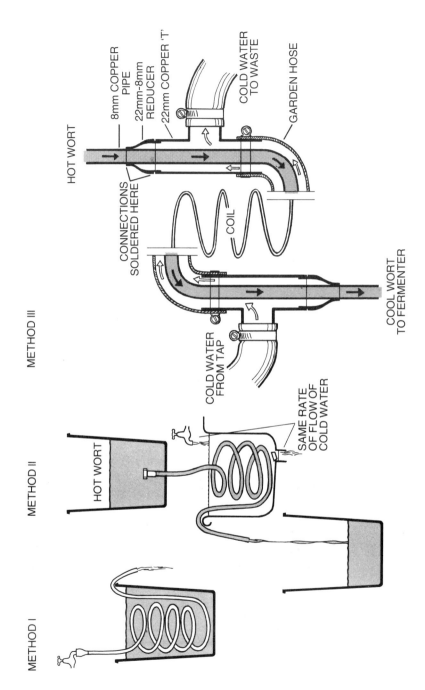

METHOD III

HOT WORT

8mm COPPER PIPE

22mm-8mm REDUCER

22mm COPPER 'T'

CONNECTIONS SOLDERED HERE

COLD WATER TO WASTE

GARDEN HOSE

COIL

COLD WATER FROM TAP

COOL WORT TO FERMENTER

METHOD II

HOT WORT

SAME RATE OF FLOW OF COLD WATER

METHOD I

Slow cooling does not however seem to retard the eventual clarity of the finished beer but we should at all times take positive steps to eliminate any risks which might impair the quality of our brews.

By far, the best approach for rapid cooling of wort is to make a coil as described below. This is a really efficient method and the temperature of wort just off the boil is reduced to 15C in 30 to 60 minutes, depending on the cold water temperature at any time of the year.

# The cooling coil

Before we go into its construction, let's look at the basic theory behind its use. There are two basic approaches to using a copper coil. If the hot wort is to flow 'through' the coil and be cooled by an external source of cold water, much better results are achieved if the coil is of a small bore so that a thin stream of hot wort is cooled by a large volume of cold water. If the coil is in a container of hot wort and cold water is passed through it to reduce its temperature, best results are achieved if the coil has a large diameter so that a large volume of cold water is passing through the wort.

The easiest copper pipe for making a cooler is 8 mm and 10 mm mirco-bore popular in central heating systems, and is readily available in any plumbers merchants or in home improvement centres. The copper pipe is easily bent into a coil to suit your choice of method but try not to get it kinked or the flow will be restricted.

Of all the methods illustrated, number one will be the easiest to construct, operate and clean after use. The other two methods are effective, but the coil does require to be flushed through with copious amounts of hot water to ensure it is thoroughly clean before and after use.

If your sink is fitted with the 'original' style of tap, a short piece of hose can be connected to the coil and then secured to the tap using the 'push-on' fitment from a hand held hair spray attachment, or alternatively use an attachment on garden hose designed for kitchen taps. Should the tap be of the 'mixer' type, it might have a male screw threaded end which is usually protected by a chrome cap, designed to take a female screw on attachment to garden hose. The attachment makes a good seal and is recommended for this system.

Method 3 is slightly more complex but it is very efficient. In this system, the hot wort flows by gravity through an 8 mm coil and is forced cooled by cold water flowing in the opposite direction through a plastic garden hose.

*The cooling coil in action.*

To make this type of coil you will require the following:

3 metres of 8 mm copper pipe
5 metres of garden hose
2 × 22 mm 'capiliary' copper 'T' pieces
2 capiliary reducers from 22 mm to 8 mm
4 Jubilee clips

To make the cooler, lay out 3 metres of garden hose and place the copper pipe inside it. Now taking great care, coil them both into a compact spiral 300 to 400 mm (12 to 16 inches) in diameter. Clean all the copper surfaces to be soldered with steel wool until the copper and the ring of solder shines brightly then apply a smear of flux which will ensure a good bond between the metal surfaces when heat is applied. Push the reducer into one end of the 'T' piece and clean the copper pipe about 150 mm from the end. Treat with flux and push the pipe right through the 'T' piece and out through the reducer until the clean area of the pipe is in line with the solder ring of the reducer. Make sure all the parts fit tight, then apply heat from a small plumber's torch to all the parts to be soldered and after a minute or so watch for a silver ring of solder forming around the joint. When this happens, remove the heat and allow the copper to cool without disturbing the joints which will damage the seal. Now repeat the process at the other end.

The hose might require to be cut back a little and then secured to the 'T' piece with a Jubilee clip. The remaining 2 metres of hose are used to supply the cooler with cold water and allow it to run to waste. The waste outlet should be fitted with a garden hose tap, which should be controlled so that the back pressure fills up the hose completely but still allows a good steady flow of water.

# 18 Fermentation

Fermentation is not simply a case of pitching yeast and leaving it to get on with the job. Certain conditions have to be considered and the manner in which fermentation is carried out will effect the character and shelf life of the brew.

## Ratio of sugars

The composition of the wort will influence the flavour of the lager, its palate fullness and head retention.

Cane sugars (sucrose) are wholly utilised by yeast but as they offer nothing but alcohol, large amounts should not be used otherwise quality defects will arise.

Maltose is the principal fermentable sugar in wort and ferments much slower than sucrose, producing a steady fermentation with healthy yeast growth and sound flavours. Maltotriose ferments slower than maltose and makes an excellent conditioning sugar during the secondary fermentation. Maltotetraose and dextrin are unfermentable and remain in the lager giving it body and sweetness to balance the bitterness of the hops.

The ratio of sugars in malt extract have already been 'fixed' but the overall fermentability of the wort will alter with added sugars, malts and adjuncts.

The conditions in the mash tun will influence the ratio of sugars and a dilute low temperature mash, such as the decoction process, will generally produce a more fermentable wort and consequently a 'dry' palate in pale lagers. A thick high temperature mash on the other hand, such as an 'infusion' mash, will favour a dextrin rich wort of reduced fermentability which is ideally suited for Munchener styles of lager.

# Amount of yeast

The amount of yeast pitched to wort can have a considerable effect on fermentation and the quality of the lager. The amount of dried yeast in a sachet is usually recommended for one to six gallons. This means therefore, that there will be a greater amount of cells in one gallon than there will be in six. A high concentration of yeast will result in a rapid fermentation and although the cells bud more slowly, there is a risk of off flavours and lack of head retention from yeast autolysis if the lager is not separated from the yeast soon after fermentation.

Small amounts of yeast, such as in liquid cultures, produce much better flavours, largely because the yeast reproduces much quicker and their by-products influence more of the aromatic compounds.

# Fermentation

Yeasts should always be added to wort as a starter. I would also advise that it is added about 15C (60F) which is, you will note, somewhat higher than the pitching temperatures used in commercial brewing. During the exhaustive brewing trials for this book, I have come to the conclusion that cold pitching temperatures are likely to prove difficult for the amateur. It is much better to allow the fermentation to become well established and then gradually let the temperature cool down to around 10–12C (50–53F). This practice will depend on the time of year or if you have a spare refrigerator.

After the wort has been cooled to 15C, it should be thoroughly aerated before pitching the yeast. Replace the snap-on lid of the fermenter and fit an air-lock.

Fermentation should be visable after 12–15 hours and will become fully active during the following 24 hours. During this time the surface of the brew will become covered with a light fluffy head of yeasty foam, which will eventually form a 'rocky' head similar to a top yeast. This is sometimes dramatic, throwing up lofty peaks and forming deep troughs over the surface of the brew. This usually happens about the 3rd or 4th day after the yeast is pitched and is accelerated as the temperature creeps up to 20C (68F). The temperature of the brew should at all times be kept as low as possible. Not all the lager yeasts I have used showed this characteristic and in most cases the surface activity remained as a thick creamy white coating on top of the brew.

As fermentation proceeds, the yeast crop gradually declines, leaving a uniform wet pancake-like froth on the surface. This usually starts

113

to break up at about a specific gracity of 1.012. It is largely a matter of choice to rack into the secondary fermenter at this stage or to do it earlier, as soon as the initial surface activity declines. The advantage of racking at an early stage is that a deposit of protein debris and dead yeast cells are left behind and that a small amount of oxygen is absorbed by the wort which will sustain it through the secondary fermentation. By continuing the fermentation with a small amount of yeast, a cleaner and more aromatic lager is produced without the risk of off flavours. Fermentation will now continue at a much slower rate and surface activity is minimal. As fermentation comes to an end, practically all the yeast will have sedimented and the surface of the brew will be covered with a dark brown crinkled and broken up film of yeast.

Ideally, the secondary fermentation should be conducted in a cold place about 10C. Obviously by using a refrigerator, temperatures will remain static but if this is not possible, try and ferment the lager in as cold a place as you can find.

During the winter months, a cold fermentation can be conducted in an outbuilding although the ambient temperature will fluctuate. This is not a great problem as we are not 'lagering' the brew for clarity purposes. Do not however, remove the fermentation from a warm house to a very cold outbuilding without giving the container some insulation, otherwise the abrupt drop in temperature will stun the yeast and fermentation will cease prematurely.

When the container is moved into a very cold place, protect it by wrapping it in the boiler duvet or some other form of insulation so that the yeast is given time to adapt to its new environment.

# Refrigeration

The advantage of using a refrigerator is that the fermentation is controlled, steady and independent of ambient fluctuations. By conducting a fermentation around 10C the formation of dimethyl sulphide is encouraged and so a true lager palate is enhanced. Control of the temperature is achieved by adjusting the temperature control knob and by removing or replacing the door of the small freezer compartment. It is also a good idea to remove the meat tray from underneath the freezer compartment as this will allow a better chilling downdraught.

When you first commission your fridge, just turn on the control knob until you hear the thermostat 'click', allow the temperature to stabilise and note the temperature.

*A vigorous 'primary' lager fermentation.*

Next, determine a range of settings which will allow a cool fermentation of about 15C, 12–10C and finally the setting which will drop the temperature to just above freezing.

To use a refrigerator in this way, remove all the shelves including the plastic bottom drawer and make a strong support to replace the drawer so the container will sit stable.

If a pressure barrel is used as a secondary fermenter, it will not be possible to fit an air-lock to vent the fermentation gas. Venting therefore, can either be manual, by cracking open the cap, or automatic, by means of the pressure relief valve, should it be possible to have it fitted. Should venting be achieved by a relief valve, it is still a wise precaution to check the container each day to ensure all is well and there is not an excessive build up of pressure.

When a polypin is being used as a secondary fermenter, the gentle rise in gas pressure is simply vented by opening the tap. Do this just to vent off the initial high pressure but do not deflate the container altogether as a slight build-up of $CO_2$ is desirable in retaining as much dissolved gas as possible.

When you decide to bottle or cask, it will be found much easier to remove the cube from the refrigerator if it is sitting on a strong flat piece of wood. This will make a steady platform for the cube which should still be in its cardboard box, so that it does not flex and disturb the sedimented solids.

The 'Drafty Five' is a container similar to a polypin except that it is fitted with a pressure relief valve. Venting is therefore automatic but the cube still retains a little back pressure. Because the cube sits in the draw-off position, it is possible to bottle direct from the refrigerator. Obviously it is not possible to cask direct from the refrigerator unless it is raised on some support or a workbench.

When using the refrigeration techniques, finings *should not* be necessary.

# Lagering

Lagering in a refrigerator should be considered if the brew is to be bottled and served chilled from your (wife's!) refrigerator. When you are satisfied that the secondary fermentation is finished, reduce the temperature of the refrigerator gradually over a few days to just above freezing point and maintain this for four weeks. During this period the polyphenol and

*A controlled fermentation in a refrigerator*

protein chill-haze factions precipitate out of solution. Once the beer is racked to leave the deposits behind the lager can be chilled without the risk of further haze appearing.

# 19 Beer finings

As not every home brewer will have a refrigerator to lager and clarify their brew, we should consider the time honoured process of clarifying beer with 'finings'.

Given time, yeasts will eventually sediment but because they are so microscopically small their weight does not encourage them to drop out of solution quickly. As long as yeasts are active, its electrical charge makes them repel each other and this also encourages them to remain in suspension longer. A beer which is slow to clear is not altogether a bad thing as long as the quantity of yeast is slight, for as long as the yeast is active, it will seek out the last traces of oxygen which might otherwise cause off-flavour. However, should the amount of yeast be fairly heavy and it is not separated from the beer, the quality of the brew will suffer from the effects of yeast autolysis, resulting in a short shelf life and poor head retention. Thus we can see that it is desirable to separate the brew from the bulk of the yeast before we bottle or barrel it.

There are two types of beer findings suitable for the amateur.

## Isinglass

Isinglass finings are made from the lung and sometimes the grills of tropical fishes and less common now, the sturgeon from Russian rivers.

The lungs are cut from the fish, dried and shredded and end up looking like fibreglass. To make it into a solution suitable for fining beer, it is first 'cut' in a diluted solution of acidified water treated with $SO_2$ to prevent the growth of bacteria. The solution is eventually filtered to remove any pieces of skin and other matter, to produce a viscous colourless substance which resembles wallpaper paste.

The isinglass solution carries a 'positive' charge and because the molecules are large, the charge is spread over a wide area and attracts a greater number of 'negatively' charged yeasts. The electrical charges nutrilise each other and so the yeast cells no longer repel each other. The combined weight of the isinglass and the attached yeast cells is sufficient to overcome gravity and a rapid sedimentation occurs leaving the brew clear within 48 hours.

# Using isinglass

Isinglass finings should be added at the end of fermentation. Do this gently but in a circular fashion to avoid an unnecessary uptake of air. Leave the brew alone and it should be quite clear of yeast within 48 hours. Should you wish to check on the action of the finings, draw off a sample as soon as they have been stirred in and keep the sample in a small bottle beside the fining container. The clarity in the test sample should show positive signs of clearing within 30 minutes. Don't forget, this only confirms that the finings are working and because the cells have a shorter distance to fall, the test sample will clear much quicker than the bulk beer.

For the reasons not yet fully understood, isinglass finings work best if the temperature is rising and is most effective between 13–15C (56–58F). Such close temperature control is likely to prove difficult for the amateur. Good results however, can be achieved by bringing the lager in from the cold and when the temperature reaches about 12C (53F), stirring in the finings and leaving in a warm place so that the brew warms up a little to achieve quick clarification.

The advantage of using isinglass is that it promotes foam stability and its fining action removes 'lipids' and wort 'fats' and so enhances head retention.

Prepared isinglass finings are readily available in home brew shops sold as 'liquid beer finings', the dosage is stated on the label and should be closely followed.

Dried isinglass is less common, but it is available to amateurs and should be prepared as follows.

# Dried isinglass

Dissolve 5 grammes ($\frac{1}{8}$ oz of 2 tsp) of tartaric acid in a 1.5 PET lemonade bottle with 375 ml ($\frac{3}{4}$ pint) of water at 12C (53F).

Add 10 grammes ($\frac{1}{4}$ oz or one dessertspoon) of dried isinglass and shake the bottle vigorously to thoroughly mix the ingredients. It is a bit troublesome trying to get the shredded isinglass through the small opening, but the alternative is to find a wide necked jar which can hold 1.5 litres.

Leave the bottle in the refrigerator for three days and during this time the acid will 'cut' the isinglass into a gelatinous fluid. The bottle should be given a good shake each day and it is important not to let the temperature rise above 16C (61F).

After three days, pour the solution into a liquidiser and run for up to 2 minutes in thirty second bursts. Return the solution to the bottle and place in the fridge for 5 minutes.

Add a further 125 ml (5 fluid ozs/8 tbsp) of cold water to the mixture and liquidise for another 30 seconds.

Add a further 4 × 125 ml lots of cold water at 5 minute intervals, liquidising for 30 seconds between additions. Place the solution in the refrigerator between mixings to ensure the temperature does not rise above 16C. The volume of the finings should now be 1 litre (1¾ pt).

When mixing is complete, add 4 campden tablets to bring the $SO_2$ level up to about 900 mg/ltr, the amount that is required to prevent bacteria attacking the isinglass.

The dosage of finings from the made up solution is about 125 ml to 250 ml for 23 litre brews. (¼ to ½ pint per 5 gallons).

Isinglass retains its fining action for about one month provided it is stored properly. Isinglass is very sensitive to temperature and should ideally be stored between 10-15C (50–60F) and under no circumstances should its temperature be allowed to rise above 20C (68F) or it will quickly be denatured into gelatine.

# Gelatine

This is commonly sold as 'dry' beer finings and is the alternative to isinglass.

It is produced from animal tissue such as calfs heels. During fining, it combines with tannins and yeasts to form a coagulate which will sediment. It is not as effective as isinglass and the brew might take a few days to clear bright. On the credit side, it is readily obtainable and is not sensitive to temperature once it is made up as a solution.

To prepare the finings, place 250 ml (½ pint) of 'cold' water in a small saucepan and sprinkle on the contents of two 11 gram sachets. Always add gelatine 'to' the liquid and never the other way round or mixing problems might occur. Stir the mixture as the granules are being

121

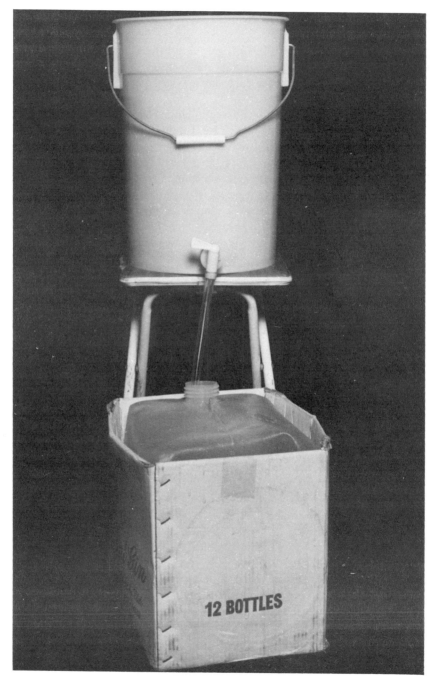

**12 BOTTLES**

*Racking beer into the fining container using an extension tube.*

added until they are fairly well dissolved. Warm the mixture gently to encourage the granules to dissolve but at no time allow the solution to boil or its fining ability will be impaired. The warm viscous solution should be pre-mixed with a little beer and then gently roused into the brew.

# 20 Bottled lager

Bottled lager is an excellent alternative to draught and I find it very handy during the summer months as the bottles can be given a quick chill in the refrigerator which enhances the lagers thirst-quenching qualities.

## Type of bottles
### PET (Poly-Ethylene-Terephallate)

These plastic beer bottles are becoming popular in the take home trade from off-licences and supermarkets, and can usually be collected from friends and neighbours in return for a few pints! They are perfectly safe for home brewed beer as long as the recommended priming rates are not exceeded. They can take a knock without becoming damaged and as they are pliable, it is easy to test if the primings have worked by just squeezing the bottle. They are also excellent 'carry-kegs' for taking beer to parties and this is discussed later.

The disadvantages are they slowly absorb oxygen and lose condition over a period of time, and are not recommended therefore, for long term storage or beer quality will suffer.

The common sizes are 1.5 and 2 litres.

## Glass beer bottles

By far, the best choice is to acquire genuine beer bottles. They are reasonably priced in home brew outlets and with a little care, give years of service. They are usually coloured green or brown which will offer the lager some protection against the actinic effects of sunlight. Light lagers are particularly prone to the effects of light and acquire the so-called 'lightstruck' or 'sunstruck' flavour.

For a real professional finish to our brews, these bottles are a must!

There are a variety of glass bottles available to the home brewer. I have a considerable number of the old-fashioned screw-stoppered bottles which are now becoming very difficult to acquire.

Keeping a good stock of washers for the stoppers might also pose a problem, but in this case, buy a short length of rubber tubing about 1 cm (½″) in diameter and cut it into 6 mm (¼″) strips which can be used as washers.

The most common type of beer bottle however, is the rim sealed type closed by a crown cap. The contents on the label of these bottles are now quoted in metric terms but the actual bottle size is roughly on par with the old imperial measures and therefore the same number of bottles are required for a 23 litre and 5 gallon brew. They are increasingly becoming available in a variety of shapes as the brewing companies and more so, the supermarket chains struggle to compete with each other.

With the upsurge of interest in imported beers, home brewers can now collect continental bottles closed with the 'swing-stopper', which used to be popular for sealing lemonade bottles in Britain until the 1950's.

275 ml or ½ pint sizes should also be collected as they are best suited for strong lagers and Bock beers.

For a 23 litre brew you will require:

15 × 1.5 PET bottles, or
12 × 2 litre PET bottles, or
40 × 1 pint bottles, or
80 × ½ pint bottles

# Closures

The rim sealed bottle is closed with a crown cap which is a saucer shaped disc with a serrated edge and a soft plastic insert. They are applied with a female hand held punch or a double handed lever type applicator. The latter is to be preferred as a much gentler pressure is applied without the risk of damaging the bottle. A small magnet holds the cap in position during sealing.

Plastic re-seals are an alternative to crown caps although they are not in my view suitable for long term storage as a loss of condition occurs over a period of time. They are easily applied with 'thumb' pressure and should fit tightly. Any which can be turned freely when fitted to the bottle should be rejected as it will leak under pressure. An early indication that a good seal has not been achieved, is the observance of a few small bubbles on the surface of the beer clinging to the side of the bottle. If you watch long enough you may catch an impudent bubble scurrying to the surface! Any bottle affected in this way should have a new cap fitted or the contents drunk on the spot!

A number of commercial beers are sealed in bottles, closed with an external aluminium cap. These caps usually present no problems but they are prone to leakage as each one is crimped to the exact shape of the screw thread on the bottle. Consequently, you might find that some of them will not seal as the caps have become mixed up during cleaning. Should any become damaged they should be replaced with new ones which are available in home brew shops. The washers on swing-stoppers should be checked and replaced regularly.

# Cleaning the bottles

Make sure the bottles to be filled are spotlessly clean and sterile and check each one carefully for chips around the rim which will not give a good seal. Reject any that are chipped or cracked as they are unsafe and might not withstand the high pressure generated by the primings.

A good idea is to acquire a couple of plastic crates in which to store your bottles. This will make cleaning, priming, filling and storing easier and much more tidy.

# Priming

Primings are a small dose of sugar added to each bottle on which the yeast will act to produce the conditioning gas that gives bottled lager its zest, sparkle and sparkling white creamy head.

The following amounts should be used and on no account should these quantities be exceeded, or a dangerous build-up of gas will result.

|  |  |  |
|---|---|---|
| 275 ml | (½ pint) | ¼ level teaspoon |
| 550 ml | (1 pint) | ½ level teaspoon |
| 1.5 litres | 1.5 level teaspoons | |
| 2.0 litres | 2.0 level teaspoons | |

Have the clean bottles in the crate and with a bowl of white sugar in one hand funnel and appropriate spoon size in the other, proceed to dose each bottle. Be methodical in this, by moving from left to right or up and down to ensure that all the bottles are primed and much more important that not one of them receives a double dose!

# Preparing the lager

Lager for bottling can be prepared in several ways.

Most beginners bottle their brews direct from the primary fermenter, but this method should be shunned. Despite the fact that lager yeasts sediment during fermentation, there will still be a considerable amount of yeast in suspension, resulting in a heavy bottle sediment giving off flavours and a short shelf life.

If you have not yet required a secondary fermenter, add 2 Campden tablets to the brew after fermentation is over to protect it against infection and leave it for 48 hours. During this time a considerable amount of yeast will drop out and the bottles sediment will be moderate.

# Standard method

When fermentation is over, rack the beer into a secondary container such as a polypin or another fermenter with a snap-on lid, add your choice of finings and allow the lager to rest for at least 48 hours. After this period, the lager should look reasonably clear with just a hint of opalescence and the resulting bottle sediment will be very light.

This method can be improved on if the lager is left to rest for a few more days when it looks clear. Now remember, yeasts are invisible to the naked eye and although the lager 'looks' clear, it will still contain an adequate amount of yeast cells in suspension to act upon the priming sugar. It takes a little longer for the lager to come into condition with this method but the sediment is only just visible and the brew has better keeping qualities.

# Advanced method

When you are satisfied that fermentation has finished, rack the brew into a secondary container and stir in the finings. Leave the brew to rest until it is absolutely clean of yeast and then gently rack it into another container which might be the original fermenter.

127

To bring the brew into condition add priming sugar *'and'* some yeast and this is added in the form of 'krausen' wort. Krausen wort is basically a yeast starter and the following tables give you the correct amount to be added.

Stir in the krausen wort and leave the yeast to adapt to its new environment and when it shows positive signs of fermentation, the brew should be bottled. Remember, when adding krausen wort the bottles *'should not'* be primed!

This method produces a first class clean tasting lager with just a hint of bottle sediment.

An alternative approach is to dose each bottle with krausen wort and fill the bottles with the clear beer.

## Krausen wort

| Water (18C) | + Sugar | + Yeast | Added to vol |
|---|---|---|---|
| 250 ml | 60 g | 1 tsp | 23 ltr |
| 200 ml | 50 g | $\frac{3}{4}$ tsp | 18 ltr |
| 150 ml | 40 g | $\frac{1}{2}$ tsp | 13.5 ltr |
| 100 ml | 25 g | $\frac{1}{4}$ tsp | 9.0 ltr |
| 50 ml | 12 g | $\frac{1}{8}$ tsp | 4.5 ltr |

Add 10 ml (2 teaspoons) per litre

| Water (68F) | + Sugar | + Yeast | Added to vol |
|---|---|---|---|
| 10 fld oz | 2 oz | 1 tsp | 40 pt |
| 8 fld oz | 1 oz | $\frac{3}{4}$ tsp | 32 pt |
| 6 fld oz | 1 oz | $\frac{1}{2}$ tsp | 24 pt |
| 4 fld oz | 1 oz | $\frac{1}{4}$ tsp | 16 pt |
| 2 fld oz | oz | $\frac{1}{8}$ tsp | 8 pt |

Add 5 ml (1 teaspoon) per pint

# Refrigeration techniques

Beer which has undergone lagering in a refrigerator, should be clean of yeast and treated with krausen wort.

An interesting technique is to condition the lager in a pressure barrel and condition it in the refrigerator and bottle 'bright' lager, completely free of yeast.

This is an advanced method which works really well and is ideally suited with PET bottles for social occasions.

After the secondary fermentation is complete, clear the beer of all yeast with finings and treat with krausen wort. Leave the barrel in a warm place for a few days until the beer comes into condition. Pre-set the refrigerator to around 12C (53F) and place the barrel in the refrigerator. Allow a few days at this temperature for the yeast to get acclimatised to the cold and then gradually over the next week, lower the temperature to just above freezing and maintain this for the next couple of weeks. This is basically the lagering technique previously described.

During this time the conditioning gas will become well dissolved in the beer and will remain in solution during the bottling. Depending on the type of pressure barrel, it might not fit inside the standard sized refrigerator if the $CO_2$ transmission valve is fitted. In this case a blank cap should be fitted and if the secondary fermentation is over before the primings are added, the barrel should not be under any undue stress.

After conditioning and lagering are over, remove the barrel from the refrigerator and place it on a worktop or whatever, ready for bottling. Gently crack open the cap until a slight hiss of escaping gas is heard. As the barrel is venting, fit a short length of tubing to the tap so that it reaches the bottom of the bottle.

Have the bottles to be filled beside the barrel. I find it much easier to sit on a stool during the bottling and by doing so, I can control the barrel tap and any fobbing which might occur.

Once the barrel is fully vented, remove the cap and place the bottle up the tube until it touches the bottom. Slowly open the tap and allow the bottle to gently fill up from the bottom to reduce the amount of fobbing and uptake of air. Fill the bottle until the beer reaches the rim and then slowly withdraw it. Watch the air space as you do so and make any adjustments to leave an air-space of about 2 cm ($\frac{3}{4}$"). As soon as the bottle is correctly filled, it must be capped immediately to prevent an unnecessary loss of condition.

Taps fitted to the original design of pressure barrel had a narrow

130          *Bottling using an extension tube to control fobbing.*

outlet and a little hole bored on the body at the front. This allowed the narrow outlet to drain free quickly. More recent designs have a larger tap outlet and so a vent hole is not necessary. However, for this technique, a drain hole is necessary to afford better control over the bottling, with quick draining of the beer in the tube.

# Conventional bottling

The beer container should be about worktop height for easy filling.

## Syphoning

Syphoning is a quick method of filling bottles and I suspect that the majority of home brewers use this approach. As the distance between the level of the beer in the container and the outlet of the syphon increases, so does the rate of flow of beer. Keep this point in mind as it is useful in controlling the flow of beer. Have the bottles in their crate on the floor and fill each one to within 2 cm to 2.5 cm (³/₄ to 1 inch) of the rim with bottles sealed with a crown cap or aluminium external screw cap. With internal screw-stoppers, the distance is from the surface of the beer to the bottom of the stopper. The air-space refers to the standard 1 pint or approximate half litre size. The air space therefore, should be reduced a little for smaller bottles and increased to not more than 28 mm or 1 inch for lager onces.

It is desirable to fill each bottle with the minimum of turbulence to prevent an unnecessary uptake of air, which will affect the brew. Light lagers in particular are prone to off-flavours after contact with air and acquire a sort of 'soggy-cardboard' flavour with maturation.

When filling the bottles, keep the syphon at the base of the bottle and as it fills up from underneath the surface of the liquid, fobbing is kept to a minimum. As the level approaches the top of the bottle, raise it so that the flow of beer almost stops. (Don't raise it too far or the beer will br drawn back into the container!) Slowly remove the bottle from the syphon by lowering it gently until the end of the tubing is just above the surface of the beer. Now make final adjustments until the correct air-space is achieved. Place the filled bottle to one side, slip your finger over the end of the tubing to stop the flow of beer and now move on to the next bottle.

Should you decide to fine your brew in a pressure barrel or Drafty Five, it will be much simpler if you fit a short length of tubing to the tap as previously described.

# Capping and labelling

Screw-stoppers, crown caps and plastic reseals should be given a brief soak in a sterilising solution before being applied.

Despite attempts at minimising fobbing, some agitation is inevitable and some condition will come out of solution. This is not a bad thing as the heavy $CO_2$ will collect at the neck of the bottle and displace the

*Sealing bottles with a crown capper.*

air there which will afford the brew some protection from developing off flavours during storage.

Seal the bottles with the appropriate closure, invert each one and give it a good shake to help dissolve the priming sugar. Wipe each bottle with a soft cloth dampened with some sterilising solution and store the bottles at room temperature for about one week.

Finally, mature the brew in a cool place which should ideally be about 10–12C (50–53F). Final maturation should not be hurried and best results are obtained when the lager rests for about four to eight weeks. During this time, the yeast sediments firmly, the condition dissolves more finely in solution and flavour and head retention are improved.

An attractive label puts the finishing touches to all efforts and although many attractive designs are available in home brew shops, many home brewers design their own.

Some means of identifying the contents of bottled beer is useful, particularly if you bottle several brews. Most home brewers use the various colours of crown caps to do this and keep a reference in their brewing log of the results of tastings and other important aspects of the brew.

# 21 Draught lager

By far, the majority of home brewers prefer draught to bottled beer and the home brew trade has responded magnificently by producing over the years a fascinating variety of draught beer containers.

## Boot's aluminium pressure barrel

This is an advanced home brew barrel designed on the same principles as a commercial keg. The barrel is made for Boots by Alumasc Ltd., who are a leading supplier of equipment to the brewing industry. The body of the barrel is made from two deep drawn halves of a very tough aluminium alloy, centre-welded around the belly.

Subsequent pressings put in the tap hole, the bottom pressure dome and the shoulder reinforcement. Finally, the filler neck is welded on which makes an excellent base for an effective seal between cap and barrel and unlike plastic barrel necks, it is not prone to impact damage which can make sealing difficult. Internally, the barrel is lined with an epoxy resin providing a tough glass-like surface which is inert and will not taint the beer in any way. The exterior is finished with a polyester coating and makes an attractive and easy-to-clean finish.

The tap is a particularly good feature of the free-flow type and the flow of beer through the tap is smooth and uninterrupted due to the crevice-free internal surfaces.

The cap is a single moulding which incorporates a carrying handle and several important safety devices built in. The safety pressure relief valve operates as soon as the pressure reaches 1.1 kg/sg cm (15 psi) and works on the same principle as commercial equipment. It is very efficient and under test, venting the entire contents of 250g $CO_2$ bottle safely and without difficulty. A baffle is fitted at the $CO_2$ inlet channel which prevents the gas impinging directly onto the beer which might freeze up the safety valve. There are holes just below the main seal of the cap which will vent off internal pressure should the cap be removed while the barrel is still under pressure. The cap has a facility to take the Boots automatic and bulk $CO_2$ gas injection systems.

# Pressure barrels

These are the original style of draught containers designed with a wooden cask-like appearance. They are made from heavy duty polythene by a blow-moulding method and are available in a variety of colours and designs at a price to suit everyone's pocket.

The original design of pressure barrel is still as popular as ever, although the latest models might differ slightly in some detail. They are closed with a narrow cap which will accept a $CO_2$ transmission valve or automatic injector system. The tap is positioned at the base and might be a screw on-off type of the conventional swivel type. They are sold under various trade names but are manufactured by only one or two companies and sizes range from 9, 15 and 25 litres (2, 3 and 5.5 gallons).

# Boots/brewcraft

These are identical pressure keg-shaped containers of about 25 litres capacity. The operating pressure should not exceed 1.1 kg/sg cm and the automatic $CO_2$ injector system recommended for these barrels will ensure that this pressure is not exceeded. They are sealed with a wide cap which makes them easy to clean and a $CO_2$ transmission valve *and* a pressure gauge can be fitted. The barrels are sold with a comprehensive instruction leaflet which covers their use in some detail.

# Rotokeg

A robust bulbous container made from strong translucent polythene. It is fitted with a high tap and closed with a wide cap and has a capacity of about 28 litres and so will take a 23 litre brew with ease. There is ample ullage therefore in which to store the excess conditioning gas.

# Beersphere (Hambleton bard)

A container which looks similar to the Rotokeg and has roughly the same capacity. Its wide sealing cap offers all the benefits previously described and is fitted with a high tap.

# Supercask (Hambleton bard)

An exceptionally good and robust container with a capacity of 30 litres. It is designed to withstand constant pressure well above the operating pressure of 1.1 kg/sg cm. One interesting point is a special 'tilt' feature which lifts the barrel slightly forward so that all the contents can be drawn off. The barrel cap is also interchangeable with other Hambleton pressure systems. The container is guaranteed for 5 years.

# Weltonhurst kingkeg

This is a super container with a capacity of 26 litres. It has a high tap and a wide sealing cap. The 'junior' model is equally robust with a capacity of 15 litres and a tap at the bottom.

# Saffron superkeg

A strong and well made container with a capacity of 26 litres. It has a wide sealing cap, easy-grip moulded handles and a 'mid' high tap. A contents scale is embossed on the plastic body and the barrel is guaranteed for 5 years.

The 'Econokeg' is designed along the same high standards but is intended for the budget end of the market.

# Float take-off system

The float take-off system is just a polyvinal tube connected to the tap outlet and a float which keeps the other end of the tube just below the surface of the beer. It is an optional piece of equipment for barrels with a base tap, but absolutely necessary for containers with 'mid' or 'high' taps.

The advantage of a high tap, is that the container can be left sitting on the floor where it is cooler and beer can still be drawn off. The advantage of the float take-off is that clear beer can be drawn off from the top of a brew which is slow to clear. Also, as no yeast sediment collects at the tap outlet, there is no risk of it being drawn through to cloud the beer.

The only disadvantage of this system in my view, is that it encourages home brewers to sup immature beer and does nothing to encourage them to learn the correct use of beer finings.

# $CO_2$ Injector systems

These are safe and reliable systems which provide an inert atmosphere in the ullage of a barrel, ensuring the beer remains in a fresh and lively condition.

The type fitted to Weltonhurst Kingkegs is particularly good as the injector fitted to the $CO_2$ cylinder is simply pushed into the opening on the transmission valve. $CO_2$ enters the barrel in short puffs every time the cylinder is pressed down. As there is no mechanical coupling, there is no risk of the device 'freezing-on' due to the chilling effect of high pressure $CO_2$ rapidly reducing to atmospheric pressure. Also, because it is a push fit seal, the back pressure from the flow of gas is continually trying to force the cylinder off the transmission valve and so it is virtually impossible to inadvertently over-pressurise the barrel.

The gas enters the barrel by burbing out from underneath a rubber washer fitted on the underside of the transmission valve, which immediately contracts over the entry hole as soon as the flow of gas stops. The pressure safety relief valve works in the same manner but the rubber washer is fitted over the escape port situated on the topside of the valve.

Rotokegs are fitted with a transmission valve which accepts a screw-threaded injector. The transmission valve is designed so that the high $CO_2$ pressure enters the barrel through a minute opening and in the unlikely event of a 'freeze-on' situation occurring, the excess gas is *'immediately'* vented off by the safety relief valve. The pressure safety relief valve is fitted separately and has several desirable features.

It works in a similar fashion to a pressure cooker indicator with a colour coded gauge which indicates the pressure required and also if it reaches excessively high levels. The valve has two openings and when the pressure creeps up a little too much, the first opening gently vents off the excess gas. Should the rise in pressure be rapid and approach dangerous levels, the second vent comes into play and because the two vents have a combined area which is greater than the entry port on the transmission valve, it is impossible to force more gas into the barrel than is leaving it.

Hambleton Bard produces a compact transmission valve system with a 'screw-on' injector which is an integral part of the $CO_2$ cylinder. As the cylinder is screwed on, the tightening pressure opens a valve and allows the gas to flow into the barrel. It is advisable not to exceed a one second burst of gas for safety and economic reasons. Any excess gas however, which enters the barrel is immediately vented off by the pressure relief valve hidden behind an aluminium collar on the top side of the transmission valve.

# $CO_2$ cylinders

Each barrel manufacturer usually markets a gas cylinder for their own particular system. Some types are however, interchangeable with other makes and this is something you should discuss with your local home brew retailer to help you make the right choice. The sizes of the cylinders vary from 145 grams to 300 grams, the larger sizes being proportionally cheaper.

Cotec International (part of the Metal Box Company) have recently marketed a reliable $CO_2$ cylinder of 300 grams capacity. It is a 'push-fit' type, designed for use with most makes of transmission valves and incorporates a fail-safe burst disc.

# Boots/brewcraft

Both companies use the design of 'automatic' $CO_2$ injector system, which uses the standard 8 gram cartridge.

The system works on a pressure and spring arrangement which keeps the pressure in the barrel at a fairly constant 0.7 kg/sg cm (10 psi).

When a barrel is under the initial high pressure produced by the sugar primings, the back pressure aided by the spring keeps the piston in the closed position and so no gas can flow from the cartridge. When the pressure in the barrel drops, the high pressure in the cartridge overcomes the resistance of the spring and so gas flows into the barrel. As the pressure in the barrel builds up again, the pressure in the piston chamber equalises on both sides of the piston and so allows the spring to force the piston into the closed position. As long as beer is drawn from the barrel, the system will work automatically.

138          The injector is supplied with a detailed instruction leaflet.

# Float take-off

The float take-off is an optional piece of equipment for barrels with a base tap but it is an absolutely necessary and integral part of a draught container which has a 'mid' or 'high' tap. The advantage of a high tap is that the container can be left sitting on the floor where it will be slightly cooler and beer can still be drawn off.

The advantages of a float take-off are that clear beer can be drawn off from the surface of the brew as it slowly clears. No yeast sediment collects at the tap outlet and so there is no risk of yeast being drawn through to cloud beer.

The disadvantages in my view, are that the float device encourages home brewers to sup immature beer and avoid the correct use of finings.

# Pressure gauge

By using the gauge with an injector, gives the brewer very accurate control over the correct dispensing pressure at which the beer runs well, producing a good sparkle and head and gentle puffs of gas from the injector should maintain this with the maximum efficiency and economy of gas.

# Lager for draught

Lager should not be barrelled direct from the primary fermenter as the yeast sediment will be far too heavy. This will affect the flavour of the brew, its head retention and shelf life. The tap too, also will be choked with yeast drawn through with the beer, producing a cloudy pint. The float take-off might overcome this but it is much better to separate the beer from the bulk of the yeast before it is barrelled.

# Basic method

The lager should be allowed to rest for at least 48 hours after the secondary fermentation is finished. No finings should be added at this stage! After this short rest, the clarity of the lager should just show a slight 'mist' due to the small amount of yeast cells in suspension. It should now be barrelled and the sugar primings and finings gently stirred into the brew.

# Standard method

After the secondary fermentation is over, the brew is racked into another container and cleared of yeast by adding finings. The beer is left for several days until it is clean of yeast, then transferred into the barrel and treated with krausen wort. No further finings should be added.

# Lagering

By completing the secondary fermentation in the refrigerator, all the yeast should have sedimented and so the lager can be racked directly into the barrel. Krausen wort should be added and the brew allowed to warm up to about 15C so that it will come into condition.

It is also possible if desired, to store the lager at just above freezing for about four weeks to remove the chill-haze complexes. This should only be necessary if you intend to store and serve the brew from a refrigerator at about 10C (50F).

# Casking

To avoid an unnecessary uptake of air by the brew, the following guidelines should be followed.

After cleaning and sterilising the barrel, fit the cap and flush it out with a burst of $CO_2$ from the injector. Allow the barrel to rest for a while so that the heavy $CO_2$ sinks to the bottom and then gently crack open the tap to allow the excess pressure to vent off. Meanwhile, prepare to rack the lager into the barrel by using a syphon or short length of tubing attached to the tap on the container. Make sure the tube touches the bottom of the barrel so that the beer fills up from under a protective blanket of $CO_2$.

As soon as the barrel is filled add the krausen wort, or primings and finings stirred in, the barrel should be capped and a further squirt of $CO_2$ injected into the barrel. This will ensure an inert atmosphere in the ullage and after a short period the excess gas should be vented off to leave an adequate space for the conditioning gas to be stored.

# Priming/fining

Sugar primings or krausen wort will provide sufficient carbon dioxide to bring the lager into condition, with a little extra to expel a few pints.

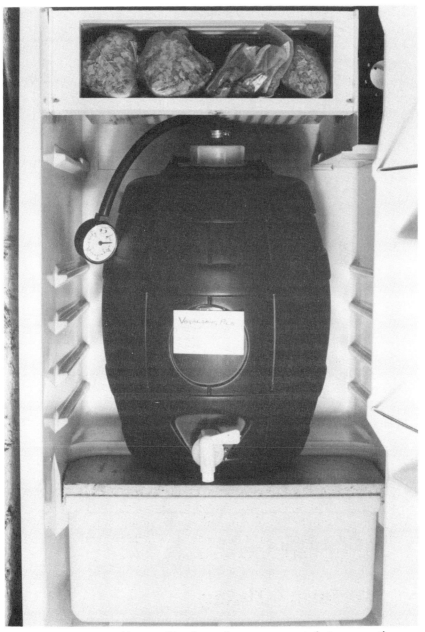

*Lagering in a refrigerator. Note the use of a pressure gauge to keep an eye on the pressure.*

The exact dose is difficult to determine as not all draught vessels are the same size. This means that with some brews a small ullage will be left in the cask and with other ones the ullage will be considerable. A small space above the beer will ensure that adequate condition remains dissolved in the lager, but a large area will store more gas at the expense of the dissolved condition in the beer. So we can see that the amount of primings must cater for the volume of the brew *and* the size of the barrel. For draught barrels up to 25 litre capacity, 3 grams per litre is quite adequate and for barrel sizes of 28 and 30 litres, 4 grams is sufficient.

## Cane sugar primings

*Cask size*

| | | |
|---|---|---|
| 9 litre | add | 30 g or 1 oz |
| 15 litre | add | 45 g or 1.5 oz |
| 25 litre | add | 75 g or 2.5 oz |
| 28 litre | add | 110 g or 3.5 oz |
| 30 litre | add | 125 g or 4.0 oz |

The above amounts are not absolute equivalents but they are well within the safe working limits of home brew draught barrels.

An alternative to cane sugar primings, is dried malt extract which has the same gravity. The maltose and maltotriose sugars in extract will produce a slower conditioning fermentation and if this is conducted at low temperatures, the tendency is for more gas to be dissolved in the beer.

Finings should only be necessary when the brew is barrelled with yeast still in suspension. If the beer is treated with krausen wort, there will not be sufficient yeast in suspension for the finings to act upon and under certain conditions this can lead to a 'lack' of clarity in the beer.

Finings and primings should be gently stirred into the beer to minimise the uptake of air.

# Conditioning

If the brew has been fermented and barrelled at ambient temperatures the yeast will readily attack the sugar primings and bring the lager into condition within a few days. However, should the beer be taken in from the cold during winter, or from a refrigerator, the temperature will be far too low for the yeast and it will simply refuse to work!

In this case, before primings are added, the beer can either be left to warm up naturally or heated up using an immersion heater.

Conditioning is best conducted about 15C (60F) which allows a positive but slow fermentation, greater absorbtion of conditioning gas and a quick drop out of yeast. Should the conditioning temperature be high, say 21C (70F), fermentation is rapid and a considerable amount of gas will be lost through the pressure relief valve as it will not readily dissolve in the beer at this temperature.

It is a good idea to move the barrel to a cold place as soon as it shows signs of positive pressure and mature for at least four weeks.

# 22 Serving lager

Bottled lager should be served at about 10C (50F) so that it is cool and crisp on the palate.

Undoubtedly, the best shaped glass for bottled lager is the graceful schooner, as it allows the condition to be released as a lively fast rising bead which collects and forms an attractive eye-catching creamy head.

When a bottle of lager has been correctly primed and chilled, the contents should not immediately gush out when opened. However, because home brewed lagers are naturally conditioned, it should be poured on opening, otherwise the continuing release of carbon dioxide will unsettle the yeast sediment and cloud the beer.

To pour a bottle of lager, have a clean and polished glass beside the bottle, prise off the bottle closure and gently run the beer down the side of the glass. Keep a steady flow and as far as practical maintain an airway at the neck of the bottle. If an adequate airway is not maintained, the air forcing itself into the bottle will produce a series of rapid ripples which will lap against the base of the bottle and bring the yeast dregs into solution.

As the glass slowly fills up, gently bring it to the vertical and pour the remainder of the lager into the centre of the glass to encourage a high frothy head. As you do this, watch out for the yeast sediment approaching the neck of the bottle and as it does so, stop pouring immediately!

Should you be pouring a large bottle into several glasses, the bottle must be kept in the horizontal position and absolutely steady, so as not to disturb the sediment by rocking the bottle as you pick up the next glass. This is a tricky manoeuvre, particularly after you have had a few!

If you have the patience, let the glass stand for a moment to let the head stabilise. Now, lift the glass to your nose and let the delicate aroma excite your nostrils; take a sip and feel the cool liquid on the palate and the pleasant tingling sensation of the $CO_2$ bubbles bursting on your tongue. Gently swallow the lager, savour its thirst-quenching flavour and its

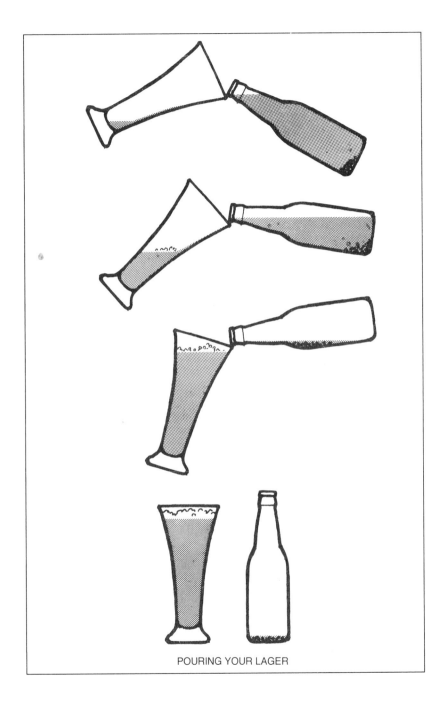

POURING YOUR LAGER

145

pleasant bitterness as it slips over the back of your throat. Now, repeat the experience . . . . . . . . . . . . . . .

Draught lager should be served about 10–12C (50–53F) to enhance its thirst-quenching qualities.

The pouring of draught lager should not be hurried, it should be done with care to ensure that it can be savoured at its best. It is a good idea to fit about 100mm (4″) of plastic tubing to the tap outlet which will give better control over the foaming of the brew.

To pour, hold the glass at an angle, close to the outlet of the tube and slowly open the tap and allow the beer to gently flow down the side of the glass. As the glass slowly fills up, keep the end of the tube under the surface of the liquid then slowly bring the glass to the vertical position. When the glass is about ⅔rds full, direct a quick jet of lager into the centre of the glass and stop pouring. Allow the head of foam to stabilise and rest for a minute or so. Now continue to gently fill up the glass with the tube at all times below the surface. When the head of froth reaches the top of the glass, stop pouring and scrape off the surplus foam, direct another quick jet of beer into the glass with the tube below the surface and allow the froth to foam over the top. Now level off the froth and let the glass stand for a moment to let the head stabilise before drinking.

Lager is traditionally served with a generous head of froth and with draught beer this is helped by the agitation set up in the beer as it passes through the tap and by the skill of the pourer as previously described. The idea is to gently shock the conditioning out of solution so that the lager acquires a soft palate, making it more quaffable and bring out a lot of the aromatic and flavouring compounds into the head.

# Using $CO_2$ injectors

Many home brewers complain about a loss of condition in draught beer drawn from a pressure barrel which gets progressively worse as the contents are consumed.

Remember that primings are only sufficient to bring the beer into condition, with a little extra pressure in the ullage to dispense a few pints. If beer is continually drawn off, the small amount of stored pressure in the ullage will be quickly spent and a situation will arise when no more beer can be drawn off. When this stage is reached, the dissolved $CO_2$ in the beer will slowly come out of solution until an equilibrium is reached. When this happens, perhaps another pint or so can be drawn off but in doing so, air will be drawn through the tap. The consequences of doing this is a disturbed yeast sediment, cloudy and oxidised beer.

The use of a $CO_2$ injector at this stage will only partially recover the situation. More beer can be drawn off, but the loss of condition cannot be restored. If the same draw-off practice is repeated, by the time half the barrel is consumed, the beer will be very flat, lifeless and with a poor flavour.

The only way to successfully overcome this problem is to maintain top pressure, slightly in excess of the dissolved condition in the beer. To do this, draw off a few pints until the initial briskness drops so that the beer is pouring well, but with a generous head of froth. Now is the time to use the $CO_2$ injector! I find it is best to give the barrel a quick squirt of $CO_2$ 'before' a pint is drawn off and another squirt immediately 'after' the glass is filled, so that the condition in the beer remains fairly constant. This practice should be carried out until all the contents have been consumed.

Automatic injectors should maintain adequate condition in the beer, but keep an eye on how well the beer is pouring and when it starts to slow down a bit, a fresh $CO_2$ cartridge should be fitted immediately.

# Keeping a cool head

Keeping a barrel of lager cool during the summer months is likely to prove difficult. I now use an old refrigerator but before I acquired one, I used a piece of hessian sacking, soaked in cold water and wrapped around the container. A piece of old woollen blanket will work just as well and it should be given a good soak in cold water, wrapped around the barrel with a couple of holes cut out so that it fits over the $CO_2$ transmission valve and tap. The blanket should be kept wet to afford adequate cooling and it would be an advantage to place little blocks of ice around the top to provide a continual seepage of ice cold water. The Boots aluminium pressure barrel should respond well to this method and the chilled water from the ice cubes will more readily draw the latent heat from the container.

# Head formation

The formation of an attractive eye-catching head on a lager depends on several factors.

For example, to produce a good foam, the beer requires the right

147

amount of conditioning gas and the right temperature. Should the beer be excessively cold, the conditioning gas will be reluctant to come out of solution. If on the other hand, the temperature is too high, the gas rapidly releases itself from the liquid and foaming is excessive. This situation leads to weak retention and very often in the case of the latter situation, cloudy beer.

Ideally, draught lager should be served at about 1C. Good head formation is only achieved with adequate maturation. It is difficult to put an exact time to the period of maturation but generally up to eight weeks is required for bottled lager and at least four weeks for draught. So much depends of course on your cellar temperature and the quality of the brew. A cool storage temperature is desirable as the $CO_2$ is more readily dissolved in the beer.

When a bottle of lager is poured, the conditioning gas rapidly expands as its pressure equalises to that of the atmosphere and as it does so it rises rapidly to the surface of the liquid, eventually colliding and collecting on the surface of the beer forming the froth or head. Small bubbles form more stable foams than large ones, as the beer drains from them much more slowly. Large soapy-like bubbles are usually the result of inadequate maturation or the beer being served at the wrong temperature. Foam drainage is rapid and the formation of the head is unstable. Draught beer correctly poured should produce adequate head formation as practically all the conditioning gas is agitated out of solution. By pouring a pint of draught lager as previously described, good head formation should be achieved.

The shape of the glass too will influence the formation of the head and the 'schooner' enhances this because the condition rises rapidly up through the liquid in the tall slim glass and the bubbles collect in a small area, compacting well to produce a tight knit creamy top. With wide topped jugs or glasses, the condition is released over a wider area and because the bubble does not have as great a distance to travel, the impact at the head is light. The formation of the head therefore, is weak and shallow and depending on the head retention characteristics of the beer, it might not last any length of time.

The skill applied to pouring a lager will also affect the formation of the head. Careless pouring of bottled lager will produce excess frothing and probably a cloudy beer which will go down with the discerning tippler like a lead balloon!

Once the head stabilises on a beer, the trapped $CO_2$ reflects light so that it looks sparkling white, making it eye-catching and inviting. As the colour of lagers darken, as it will in Vienna and Munich types, the bubble film restricts the flow of light and so the colour of the head portraits various attractive shades of oatmeal.

# Head retention

Head retention refers to the stability of the foam formed on pouring a beer and the time it takes for the froth to collapse. The stability of the head depends on many factors such as the bubble size. A small bubble gives greater retention because the surface to air ratio is greater than in large bubbles and as it scurries up through the liquid, it collects a greater amount of foam stabilising compounds. The strength of the skin is made up of trace amounts of sugar, gums and glycoproteins (protein with attached carbohydrate), Polypeptides (long chain amino acids) and the iso-alpha-acids from the hops all contribute to the rigidity of the foam, making it a semi-solid texture. The amounts of these substances will determine the life of each bubble and consequently the retention of the head. As the beer starts to drain out of the bubbles and in particular as the lager is supped, the iso-alpha-acids produce the cling or lacing effect on the side of the glass. Well hopped lagers should positively show this characteristic. Laymen usually judge the quality of a beer on how well the glass retains this effect.

# Faults and remedies

I should like to make it quite clear from the outset, that problems in home brewing are few and far between if attention has been paid to cleanliness and brewing techniques!

# Brew will not ferment

Fermentation might not occur for several reasons.

If the temperature of the wort is too high when the yeast is pitched, the yeast will be killed off. If it is too cold, the yeast simply will not work. It is for this reason that I always recommend the use of a starter, adding it to wort at 15C. Ideally once a fermentation takes hold, the temperature should be gradually lowered to 10–13C. If this is not possible try and keep the temperature below 18C.

From my experience, the major cause of fermentations not starting, or at worst being sluggish, is that the wort has not been adequately aerated before the yeast is added.

Always use as fresh a yeast as possible and never use old yeast or off flavours will result.

# Disease

Disease is very definitely preventible by sensible cleaning and sterilising. Home brewers are conscientious about their brewing activities and I feel anyone who has had a brew infected has been unfortunate.

Beer however, has a favourable pH and nutrient value for a host of bacteria to thrive in and so it is very important not to overlook any aspect of cleanliness.

Infections might show up on equipment as slimy moulds or dry webb-like growths. In beer, they show many characteristics ranging from turbidity, oily viscosity, rods and threads dangling in the brew. We do not need to be a bacteriologist to spot a brew which has become infected, but usually the first signs are seen when a pint is poured. Should you suspect a brew has become infected, the best course of action is to pour it down the drain and clean and sterilise all your brewing equipment and utensils.

# Flat bottled beer

Should all the bottles be flat, could it be that you forgot to prime them, or add krausen wort?

If only one or two bottles are affected, the problem is likely to be faulty closers. Always check these before bottling and ensure washers are in good repair. Check too, the shape of screw caps and the rim of the bottles to ensure they are sound.

If bottles are stored in a very cold place immediately after filling, the yeast will not work due to the cold and consequently the beer will be flat. Always 'warm condition' the bottles for a few days before maturing in a cold place.

# Flat draught beer

A pressure barrel will quickly go flat if any of the sealing washers are faulty. The cap sealing washer and $CO_2$ transmission washer should be checked regularly to ensure they are not perished and cause a slow leak.

A smear of petroleum jelly on the sealing ring on wide caps is particularly beneficial, as it helps the cap screw on smoothly! Without this lubrication, the halting and jarring movement of the cap as it is screwed on might give a false impression that it is sealing tight. If it is not, a slow escape of gas will result. It is important too, that the cap is not overtightened as this will distort the sealing ring and allow an escape of gas. Always keep a spare washer handy in case of emergencies!

The securing nuts on $CO_2$ transmission valves should not be overtightened, as this will unseat the washer and spread it out from under the nut and because it does not seal properly, a slow leak results.

These washers are shaped so that they fit exactly the shape of the transmission valve and so it is important that they are correctly fitted, otherwise a leak will occur.

# Burst bottles

Burst bottles are more likely to be suffered by the impatient beginner who just can't wait to bottle his first brew! This is caused by bottling the beer too early and the combined effects of the residual sugar in the brew, plus the added priming sugar produces a pressure which the bottle is unable to hold. Beer for bottling should be well attenuated and its specific gravity checked for stability before bottling. Primings and krausen wort should not exceed the amounts in the previous charts.

# Over-live bottled beer

A bottle of lager correctly primed and lightly chilled should not show signs of gushing as soon as it is opened. Should this happen, the cause is linked to over priming and the brew not being adequately attenuated before bottling. If the bottle is stored at too high a temperature, it will be lively and frothy with a heavy cloying palate.

If frothing is excessive, the yeast sediment will quickly rise up and cloud the beer. In such circumstances, it is likely that all bottles will be the same and they should be carefully vented and poured into a barrel. The lager should be drunk as soon as it clears as its quality is not enhanced by such treatment.

*A variety of drinking vessels collected by the author.*

# No head retention

In a well balanced recipe, there should be adequate foaming material. If a lager shows good condition rising up through the liquid, but little or no head retention, it might be due to over boiling the wort which will have precipitated too much foam forming protein. A short boiling of about 60 minutes should improve head retention, although the shelf life can in some circumstances be limited. If the lack of head retention is persistent in malt extract brews, it is a good idea to boil the hops separately for 40 minutes and then add the extract for the last 30 minutes.

A prolonged protein rest will remove too much of the head retaining properties and excessive sparging will wash through anti foaming agents. If the lager is stored on a very heavy yeast sediment for a long time, the fatty acids released by the dying yeasts will affect the stability of the foam.

Traces of grease on drinking glasses will destroy the head on a beer and so glasses should be thoroughly cleaned and rinsed out before and after use. Tasty party snacks like cheese and crisps will also affect the head on a beer as will a high level of alcohol in high gravity brews. Although in such circumstances, complaints are unlikely!

153

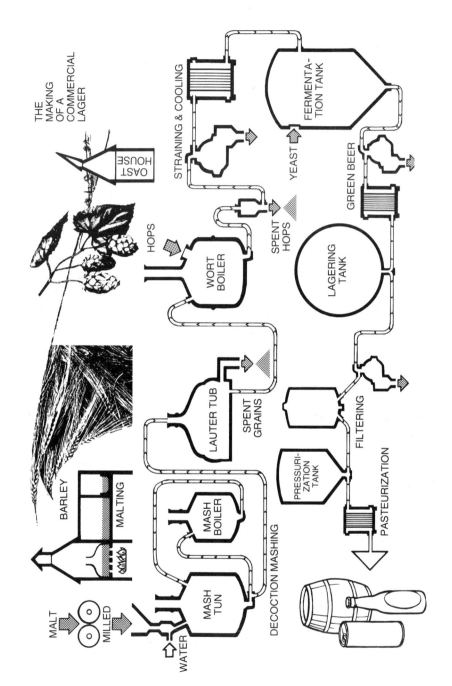

THE MAKING OF A COMMERCIAL LAGER

OAST HOUSE

STRAINING & COOLING

FERMENTATION TANK

YEAST

GREEN BEER

HOPS

SPENT HOPS

WORT BOILER

LAGERING TANK

BARLEY

MALTING

LAUTER TUB

SPENT GRAINS

FILTERING

MASH BOILER

PRESSURIZATION TANK

PASTEURIZATION

MASH TUN

DECOCTION MASHING

MALT

MILLED

WATER

154

# Glossary

**Acrospire**   The small shoot which grows under the husk in barley and eventually produces the first blade of grass. The degree of modification is judged by its length.

**Aeration**   The practice of 'rousing' air into the wort to stimulate yeast activity.

**Aerobic fermentation**   A fermentation conducted in the presence of air. It encourages yeast growth but little alcohol.

**Alcohol**   A by-product of fermentation.

**Ale**   In olden times a beer flavoured with herbs instead of hops.

**Alpha acid**   The hop resin humulon, which gives beer its pleasant bitterness when converted into iso-alpha acids.

**Alpha amylase**   The enzyme which converts starch into dextrin.

**Amino acid**   The ultimate end products of the breakdown of protein by the proteolytic enzymes.

**Anaerobic fermentation**   A fermentation conducted in the absence of air forcing the yeast to reproduce in a manner which encourages the production of alcohol.

**Attenuation**   The thinning out of the wort's density, or gravity, due to the removal of the weight of sugar during fermentation.

**Autolysis**   When the yeast cell dies its electrical charge is switched off and it is digested by its own enzyme system. As it decomposes it releases fatty acids, which can have a deleterious effect on head retention, and bitter substances which cause 'yeast bite'.

**Beta acid**   The hop resin lupulon, it does not have the same bittering power as alpha-acid.

**Beta glucan**   A substance found in the cellulose structure surrounding the wall of the starch in barley. When broken down during malting it is highly viscous and aids the foaming of beer. Too much, however, might cause problems with wort run-off during sparging and brewers add the enzyme 'bacterial beta-glucanase' to the mash tun to control it.

**Beer**   A generic term for ales, stouts and lagers brewed with hops.

**Bitter wort**   The wort separated from the hops after boiling.

**Bromates**   A substance added to grain to improve germination during malting. It suppresses the formation of dimethyl sulphide in ale malts.

**Caramel**   A colouring and flavouring substance produced by heating glucose in the presence of ammonia at 140°C. Caramel was once referred to as burnt sugar.

**Cereals**   Edible grain such as wheat, barley, rice and maize used as mash tun adjuncts.

**Chitting**   A term used to describe the early growth of the barley shoots.

**Condition**   The sparkle and freshness of palate that a beer has due to the dissolved carbon dioxide gas in it.

**'Copper'**   The wort boiler in a brewery, so named as it was traditionally made of copper. Sometimes called a kettle.

**Copper adjuncts**   Sugars and syrups added to the wort during boiling.

**Couching**   A method used in traditional 'floor' malting techniques where the barley is initially left in heaps to keep it warm and encourage growth.

**Diastase**   A collective name for all the enzymes which convert starch in sugars. i.e. alpha and beta anylase, maltase (a-glucosidase) and dextrinase.

**Dimethyl sulphide**   A sulphur related chemical which occurs naturally during malting, kilning and fermentation. It is more evident in lager than ale and contributes to the true lager palate.

**Endosperm**   The pocket of reserved starch in barley which will feed the growing shoots until they can absorb energy from the sun and soil.

**Enzyme**   Organic catalysts produced by living cells, which have the ability to change other substances whilst their own structures remain unaltered.

**Gelatine**   A protein obtained from animal tissue. It is dissolved into a viscous solution and aids the clarification of beer.

**Gibberellic acid**   A plant hormone which speeds up the cultivation of the enzyme system. It is sometimes sprayed onto barley to reduce the time of malting.

**Glycoprotein**   Protein with attached carbohydrate which assists the rigidity of beer foam and consequently assists head retention.

**Grist**   The crushed malt, or malt and adjuncts before mixing with hot water in the mash tun.

**Grits**   Raw cereals rough milled to remove the outer layers, then lightly crushed to extract the starchy endosperm. Before being added to the mash tun, grits are cooked in a mash kettle to gelatinise the starch which ensures a good starch/sugar conversion.

**ISO-alpha-acids**   during boiling the molecular structure of the alpha acids rearrange themselves and become more soluble and bitter.

**Krausening**   The practice of adding actively fermenting wort to condition and produce 'life' in dead, or flat beer.

**Lauter tun**   A mashing vessel similar to an infusion mash tun, but shallower. Wort run-off is assisted by propeller-shaped blades which slowly rotate allowing a faster wash through effect.

**Lintner degrees**   A scale used to work out the diastatic power in malt; ale malts are in the range 35–55°, some lager malts peak at 200°.

**Lipids**   Long chain fatty acids extracted from malt during mashing, from hops during wort boiling and from yeast during fermentation. An excess of lipids can have a bad effect on head retention and beer flavour.

**Liquor**   In the brewing industry, water for brewing.

**Mash tun adjuncts**   Cereals prepared as grits or flakes added to the mash tun to supplement the malt content.

**Maturation**   The period after fermentation during which yeast and proteins precipitate, subtle chemical changes take place, the beer comes into condition and acquires a smooth, clean and fresh palate.

**Meniscus**   A phenomena caused by the surface tension at the gas/liquid interface, which prevents a liquid from becoming a gas. The effect of the surface tension is to cause the liquid to rise up slightly at the side of a trial jar and the stem of the hydrometer.

**Palate fullness**   An expression used to describe the 'feel' of the beer on the tongue. Palate fullness is produced by proteins, peptides, richly flavoured substances extracted from crystal and roast malts and water treatments, particularly chlorides.

**Peptide**   The intermediate product between an amino acid and a protein. It is produced by the enzyme peptidase.

**p.H.**   The value in a measure of the hydrogen ion concentration defined on a logarithmic scale ranging from 1 to 14. Distilled water has a value of 7. Values less than 7 are acidic and values above 7 are alkaline.

**Polyphenol**   A complex group of organic compounds. They influence beer colour and flavour and react with proteins to form chill haze. Polyphenols also assist the protein 'break' during boiling and cooling.

**Protein**   An organic compound consisting of carbon, hydrogen, nitrogen, oxygen and sulphur.

**Racking**   The transferring of worts and beer from one container to another. Also called syphoning.

**Rousing**   The practice of stirring wort to aerate it or to keep the yeast in suspension. The practice of one activity usually encourages the other.

**Saccharomyces Carlsbergensis**   A bottom fermenting yeast cultivated by Hansen at the Carlsberg Laboratories in 1883. Until quite recently the name applied to all bottom fermenting lager yeasts but they are now classed as Saccharomyces Uvarum. The term Carlsbergensis, however, is still in use at the Carlsberg breweries to distinguish their own No. 1 strain.

**Saccharomyces cerevisiae**   A top fermenting yeast used in British breweries to produce ales and stouts.

**Silica**   A mineral found in the outer layer of the husk of barley. It can impart a harsh taste in beer if excessive amounts are extracted into wort by over zealous sparging of the mash.

**Sweet wort**   The wort extracted from the mash tun before it is boiled with hops.

**Torrified**   To cook, or in the case of malt, to roast.

**Trub**   Another name for the hot and cold break.

**Ullage**   The amount a cask wants of being full.

# Index

Acrospire, 9, 10
Adjuncts 'copper', 25
  Malt extract, 17, 18, 19, 20, 21, 26, 70, 71
  Barley syrup, 26, 57, 70
  Golden syrup, 26, 70
  Glucose chips, 26, 57, 70
  Glucose powder, 26, 57, 70
  Cane/beet sugars, 26, 69, 70
  Lactose, 27
  Caramel, 27
Adjuncts 'mash tun', 22
  Flaked maize, 24, 69, 70
  Flaked rice, 24, 70
  Torrified barley, 24, 70
  Torrified wheat, 25, 70
  Wheat malt, 25, 70
  Wheat flour, 25, 70
  Grits, 25
  Storage, 25
Aeration, 32, 107
Aerobic fermentation, 29
Air lock, 32, 52, 57
Ale, 35
Ale malt, 10, 14, 70
Alpha acids, 39
Alpha amylase, 84, 85
Anaerobic fermentation, 29
Autolysis, 113, 119

Bacteria, 52, 58
Barley, 8, 9, 24
Beer finings, 119
Beta amylase, 84, 85
B-glucan, 23
Bock Bier, 6, 7, 46, 81, 85
Boiling, 12, 89, 99
Brewing equipment, 52, 53, 54
Bromates, 15
Bruheat boiler, 71, 86, 87, 89, 99, 101
Burco boiler, 100

Calcium carbonate, 45, 46, 47, 105
Calcium chloride, 48, 51
Calcium phosphate, 46, 48
Calcium sulphate, 46, 47, 60, 105
Carbonates, 6, 48, 49, 105
Carbon dioxide, 1, 9, 12, 29, 34
Carlsberg, 3, 4, 5
Chlorides, 6
Cleaning, 59, 60, 61
Cleaning chemicals, 58, 59
$CO_2$ cylinders, 138
Conditioning, 142
Cooling, 12
Cooling methods, 107, 108, 109, 110, 111, 126
Cooling wort, 107
Copper, 12
$CO_2$ systems, 131, 146

Decoction mashing, 11, 83
Degrees of extract, 67, 68
Dextrinase, 84
Dextrins, 84, 112
Diastase, 9, 15, 84
Diastatic Extracts, 76
Dimethyl sulphide, 15, 114
Disease, 150
Dortmunder, 6, 46, 50, 74, 76, 80, 81
Draught containers, 134, 135, 136
Draught, cooling, 147

Electrim bin, 71, 87, 97, 99
Endosperm, 9
Enzyme, 17, 25, 28, 85

Fatty acids, 24, 153
Fermentation, 2, 3, 4, 112, 113
Fermentation vessel, 52
Fructose, 28

161

Gelatine, 121
Gibberellins, 9
Gibberalic acid, 9
Glucose, 28
Glycoprotein, 25, 149

Hansen, 4, 5
Haze, 2, 12, 92
Head formation, 147
Head retention, 23, 24, 25, 27, 68, 83, 85, 149, 153
Hop back, 103
Hops, 12, 35
 Cultivation, 35
 Picking, 36
 Drying, 37
 Disease, 38
 Parts of, 38
 Products, 39
 Cone hops, 39, 101
 Pellets, 39, 101
 Powders, 40, 101
 Extracts, 41, 101
 Oil, 41
 Storing, 43
 Goldings, 42, 43
 Northdown, 42, 44
 Challenger, 42, 44, 56
 Zenith, 42, 44
 Yeoman, 42, 44
 Target, 43, 44
 Hallertaur, 43, 44, 89
 Styrion goldings, 43, 56, 89
 Saaz, 43, 56, 89
Hot break, 47, 48, 105
Hydrometer, 62, 63, 64, 65
Hygroscopic, 21, 49

Iodine, 78
Irish moss, 104
Isinglass, 119, 120
Iso-alpha-acids, 99, 149
Isomerised hop extract, 56

Kettle, 12
Kilning, 10
Krausen wort, 128

Lactic acid, 49, 50
Lager, brewing, 8
Lager, bottled, 124
Lager, draught, 139
Lagering, 13, 116

Lager ingredients, 14
Lager, serving, 144, 145
Lager yeast, 30
Lauter tun, 12
Lintner, 76
Lipids, 24, 25
Litre, 67, 68, 69, 70

Magnesium sulphate, 48
Maltase, 84
Malt extract, 17, 26
 Production, 17
 Types, 19, 20
 Shelf life, 21
Malting, 8
Maltose, 28, 84, 85, 112
Maltotriose, 28, 112
Malts,
 Lager, 10, 14, 69, 70
 Ale, 10, 14, 70
 Wheat, 70
 Crystal, 15, 70
 Cara Pils, 15, 70
 Roast, 15, 70
 Chocolate, 16, 70
 Buying, 16
 Storage, 16
Mashing methods, 77
Melibiose, 30
Meniscus, 63
Milling, 10
Munchener, 6, 27, 45, 45, 48, 50, 74, 75, 76, 81, 85, 112

Nitrogen, 8, 9, 22

Palate fullness, 48, 83, 85
Paraflow refrigerator, 12
Peptidase, 83
p.H., 23, 46, 47, 48, 50, 85
Pilsners, 1, 2, 5, 45, 46, 48, 50, 73, 74, 76, 79, 80, 85
Pint, 67, 68, 69, 70
Polypeptides, 83, 149
Polyphenol, 25, 47, 68, 116
Polypin, 71
Potassium chloride, 48, 51
Primings, 126, 140, 142
Protease, 83, 84
Protein, 1, 9, 11, 22, 46, 47, 48, 83, 103, 118
Protein rest, 83, 85
Proteolysis, 11, 17, 83, 85

Raffinose, 30
Rainwater, 49, 50, 51
Recipes, dried extract,
  Light Pilsner, 71
  Medium Pilsner, 72
  Dortmunder, 72
  Munich Style, 73
Recipes, liquid extract,
  Pilsner 1, 73
  Pilsner 2, 73
  Pilsner 3, 74
  Dortmunder 1, 74
  Dortmunder 2, 74
  Munchener 1, 74
  Munchener 2, 75
Recipes 'diastatic' extract,
  Pilsner 1, 79
  Pilsner 2, 80
  Pilsner 3, 80
  Dortmunder 1, 81
  Dortmunder 2, 81
  Munich Style, 81
  Bock Bier, 81
Recipes from malt,
  Vogalsang Pils, 88
  Sommerbier, 90
  Friockheim Brau, 91
  Broughty Bran, 91
  Rosenmuntag Bier, 92
  Der Schutzenfest Bier, 92
  Schwarz Katze Bier, 93
  Schwarz Schwann Bier, 93
  Karlsbrau, 94
  Kiaserbrau, 94
  Vienna Style, 95
  Weizen Bier, 96
  Bavarian Maid, 96
  Dopplebock, 96
Reductones, 16
Refrigeration, 1, 2, 114, 129
Reinheitsgebot, 6
Rousing, 30

Saccharomyces,
  Carlsbergensis, 5, 30
  Uvarum, 30

Ellipsoideus, 4
Pastorianus, 4, 5
Salvator, 6
Silica, 68
Sodium chloride, 48
Sodium metabisulphate, 52
Sparging, 12, 78, 86, 89
Starch test, 78
Straining hops, 103
Sucrose, 28, 112
Sugar, 55
Sulphates, 6
Syphoning, 131

Temperature,
  Kilning, 10, 15, 16
  Mashing, 11, 77, 83, 84, 85
  Sparging, 12, 86
  Cooling, 107, 109
  Fermenting, 105, 113
  Finings, 120, 121
  Bottling, 133
  Serving, 146
Thermometer, 66
Total hardness, 49, 50

Ullage, 137, 142, 146

Water, 45
  Types, 45
  Soft, 45, 50
  Hard, 45, 50
  Temporary hard, 46, 49
  Permanently hard, 46, 49
  Treatments, 50, 51
Wurzburger, 6

Yeast, 28
  Reproduction, 28
  Classification, 29
  Types (see Saccharomyces)
  For home brew, 31
  Dried, 30, 32, 113
  Liquid, 32
  Starters, 31, 37
  Re-using 32

165

# It's taken us over 150 years to perfect our beer.

155 years ago, our founder, James Paine, started up what became a thriving country brewery.

The skills, secrets and techniques involved in making John Bull homebrew kits are the same as the ones we used to brew beer well over a century ago.

In those days it took a lot of time and hard work to brew a decent pint. Now it will take you only three to four weeks.

Our homebrew kits range from a full-bodied bitter to a pale golden Pils-Lite lager. For the more experienced, there's our Masterclass range to choose from.

Whichever kit you decide to make, you'll find our homebrew works out at around 10p a pint.

This, we think you'll agree, is a small price to pay for such perfection.

# It will take you just over 3 weeks.

## Paine's. Only the best will do.

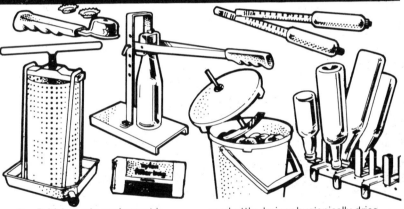